AMAZING INDIA FACTS

Terry O'Brien is an esteemed academician and an ardent quiz aficionado. He is keenly interested in kindling the quizzing instinct in people and an aptitude to develop the 3Rs of learning: Read, Record, and Recall. He is a trainers' instructor and a motivational speaker. He has penned a number of books. He is very well known for his flair for speaking and his articulating abilities in writing.

Bestsellers by the Author

CATEGORY I

Language skills for all age groups from class 3 onwards: The Little Red Book series.

CATEGORY II

For beginners: *A Child's First Dictionary* (The Little Red Book series).

CATEGORY III

To develop a love for reading among schoolchildren and also for adults, a collection of the best stories by renowned writers: The Masterpieces of World Fiction series.

CATEGORY IV

For developing quiz instinct and general awareness: The Fun Fact series—*Fun with Numbers, Fun with Riddles,* etc.; *A2Z Quiz Book; The Book of Firsts and Lasts.*

CATEGORY V

Motivational books: *The Book of Virtues* and *The Book of Motivation.*

CATEGORY VI

For overall preparation and general awareness: *The Students' Companion.*

CATEGORY VII

Teachers' reference book: *A2Z Book of Word Origins.*

AMAZING
INDIA
FACTS

TERRY O'BRIEN

RUPA

Published by
Rupa Publications India Pvt. Ltd 2016
7/16, Ansari Road, Daryaganj
New Delhi 110 002

Sales centres:
Allahabad Bengaluru Chennai
Hyderabad Jaipur Kathmandu
Kolkata Mumbai

Copyright © Terry O'Brien 2016

The views and opinions expressed in this book are the author's own and the facts are as reported by him which have been verified to the extent possible, and the publishers are not in any way liable for the same.

All rights reserved.
No part of this publication may be reproduced, transmitted, or stored in a retrieval system, in any form or by any means, electronic, mechanical, photocopying, recording or otherwise, without the prior permission of the publisher.

ISBN: 978-81-291-3989-4

First impression 2016

10 9 8 7 6 5 4 3 2 1

Printed by HT Media Ltd, Noida

Typeset by Chetan Sharma

This book is sold subject to the condition that it shall not, by way of trade or otherwise, be lent, resold, hired out, or otherwise circulated, without the publisher's prior consent, in any form of binding or cover other than that in which it is published.

'India is the cradle of the human race, the birthplace of human speech, the mother of history, the grandmother of legend, and the great grandmother of tradition. Our most valuable and most instructive materials in the history of man are treasured up in India only.'

—*Mark Twain*

Contents

Introduction   ix

1. Contours   1
2. Colours and Symbols   16
3. Dimensions   62
4. Icons   75
5. Cinematics   94
6. All Four Sides   100
7. Snippets   130

Introduction

India is a country that leaves one spellbound. It is a land that is picturesque with its alluring contrasts and striking features. 'Amazing' is the epithet that suits this incredible land that is a 34,000 years old country with a rich legend and history. One is sure to get intermingled with a collage of customary and contemporary ingredients of India. The rich rituals, distinct culture, festivals and ceremonies that India celebrates, unfold its legendary sagas.

India is bordered on the north by Nepal, Pakistan, China, and Bhutan. At one point, 'Lands End' at Kanyakumari and three seas meet—the Indian Ocean, the Arabian Sea and the Bay of Bengal. The sights, sounds, and scenery of India are unique and amazing with grandiose temples, lush paddy fields and stunning beaches. In the north, shrubland and desert create a sublime backdrop and a visit to the 'Golden Triangle' (Delhi/Agra/Jaipur/Delhi) will take your breath away. It is divided into twenty-nine states and six union territories, and has seventeen major languages with 844 dialects, making this country and its people culturally diverse.

India has always been exalted and remembered fondly as the country of symbolic colours. Its colourful culture, streets, and stories seem like pages out of an ancient folk tale. But colour, in essence, has been a large part of the Indian consciousness.

India is a land of varied culture, people and landscapes with hundreds of fairs and festivals all through the year.

In a country as diverse and culturally vibrant as India, it is the common, simple expressions of colour that hold together the multitudes of outlooks, lifestyles, and traditions. The symbolism of colour stands out and controls every aspect of life in India, be it religion, politics, festivals, or celebrations. In India, be it the north, south, west, or east, colour and culture go hand in hand.

Amazing India Facts welcomes you to the riot of colours and a labyrinth of incredible India!

Happy Reading!

Terry O'Brien

1 Contours

Indian geography is a showcase of diversity. India's landscape varies from snow-capped peaks to deserts, plains, rainforests, hills, and plateaus. India has a vast coastline of over 7000 km, and is home to some of the highest mountains of the world. It has a number of rivers that provide fertile deltas; it is also home to the barren Thar Desert. India has the second coldest place on the earth and at the same time it has places that witness temperature over 50°C in summers. This is a fascinating land. Hold your breath, amazing India will grip the imagination.

Longitudinal and Latitudinal Extents of India

India lies wholly in the northern and eastern hemispheres. Its main land extends from 8° 4' 28" N to 37° 17' 53" N latitudes and from 68° 7' 53" E to 97° 24' 47" E longitudes. The latitudinal and longitudinal extent of India is approximately the same i.e. 30°. The Andaman and Nicobar Islands extend further southwards and add to the latitudinal extent of India. The southernmost point known as the Indira Point in the Great Nicobar Island is at 6° 45' N. The latitudinal extent of India from Kashmir in the north to Kanyakumari in the south is 3,214 km. India's longitudinal extent from the Rann of Kutch in the west to Arunachal Pradesh in the east is 2,933 km.

Geographical Area of India

India has an area of 3,287,240 sq. km. It is the seventh largest country of the world after Russia (1,70,75,000 sq. km), Canada (99,76,132 sq. km), China (99,76,132 sq. km), the U.S.A. (90,72,340 sq. km), Brazil (85,11,965 sq. km) and Australia (76,82,300 sq. km). India accounts for about 2.4 per cent of the total surface area of the world. India is nearly twenty times as large as Great Britain. Many of the Indian states are larger than several countries of the world.

Kibithu

Kibithu is at the easternmost point of India. This is a tiny village located at an altitude of 11,000 feet in Arunachal Pradesh's Lohit District, bordering China's Tibet region. Kibithu is nestled on the right bank of the mighty Lohit River. It is the first settlement along the banks of Lohit River in Arunachal Pradesh after the river enters the Indian territory from China. The climate of Kibithu is cool and salubrious. The whispering pine forests, wild raspberries, beautiful flowers and majestic waterfalls set against tall blue hills add to the abundant natural beauty of Kibithu.

Kibithu witnessed some of the fiercest fights by Indian soldiers against the Chinese in 1962. But with the passage of time Kibithu is fast emerging to be a new melting point of Indo-China friendship. It offers relatively easy travel up to Chinese side.

Five Treasures of Great Snow

Kanchenjunga is the highest mountain peak in India with an altitude of 8,586 metres (28,169 feet). It is engirdled by three territories: Sikkim in the south and east, Nepal in the west, and Tibet in the north. The name Kanchenjunga is derived from the Tibetan words, 'Kanchen' and 'Dzonga', meaning 'Five Treasuries of the Great Snow', as it contains five peaks. The treasures represent the five repositories of god, which are  gold, silver, gems, grain, and holy books. The five ridges are named according to their respective directions with reference to the main peak to which they are attached.

The five peaks of Kanchenjunga are:

- Kanchenjunga Main: 8,586 m
- Kanchenjunga West: 8,505 m
- Kangchenjunga Central: 8,482 m
- Kangchenjunga South: 8,494 m
- Kangbachen: 7,903 m

Land Of The Sundari Trees

Sunderban is a unique ecosystem dominated by mangrove forests and gets its name from the Sundari

trees. Sunderban is spread over 54 islands and two countries. It is one of the last preserves of the Bengal tiger and the site of a tiger preservation project.

Sundarban is the largest delta in India. The Sundarbans are a part of the world's largest delta formed by the rivers Ganga, Brahmaputra and Meghna. They include vast tract of forest and saltwater swamp forming the lower part of the Ganges Delta, extending about 260 km along the Bay of Bengal from the Hooghly River Estuary in India to the Meghna River Estuary in Bangladesh. Sunderbans cover an area of 4,262 sq. km in India.

THE PLACE OF WILD ROSES

The word 'Siachen' means 'the place of wild roses'. Siachen glacier is the largest glacier in India; it has the distinction of being the largest one outside the polar and the sub-polar regions too. Siachen glacier is 75.6 km long and 2.8 km wide. It is the source for the 80 km-long Nubra River, a tributary of the Shyok, which is part of the Indus River system.

The Siachen glacier lies south of the great watershed that separates China from the Indian subcontinent in the extensively glaciated portion of the Karakoram. Siachen also has the dubious distinction of being the highest battleground on earth. India and Pakistan have fought intermittently since April 13th, 1984. The volume of the glacier has been reduced by 35 per cent over the last twenty years. Global warming and military activity have been cited as the main reasons for the receding of the glacier.

MANJULI

Manjuli Island in Assam is the largest river island in India. Majuli is in the Brahmaputra river, and is about 200 kilometres east from Guwahati, the capital of Assam. Majuli was formed due to course changes by the River Brahmaputra and its tributaries, mainly the Lohit. The total area of the island was 1250 sq.km but due to erosion its present area is 557 sq km.

Majuli is inhabited mainly by the tribals. Major tribes are: Mishing, Deori, and Sonowal Kacharis. Major languages spoken in Majuli are Assamese, Mishing, and Deori. The island has twenty-three villages with a population of 150,000 and a density of 300 persons per square km.

Government of Andaman and Nicobar Islands

Andaman and Nicobar

Andaman and Nicobar Islands with an area of 8,249 sq km is the largest union territory in India. The Andaman and Nicobar Islands are situated between 6° and 14° North Latitude and 92° and 94° East Longitude. The group of 572 islands / islets is located in the Bay of Bengal, 1,255 km from Kolkata and 1190 km from Chennai. The entire chain of island consists of two distinct groups of islands. The Great Andaman group of islands in the north is separated by the Ten Degree Channel from the Nicobar group in the south. The

Andaman group of islands is divided into three main groups viz., North Andaman, Middle Andaman and South Andaman. Little Andaman is separated from the Great Andamans by the 50 km wide Duncan Passage. The Nicobar group of islands consists of seven big and twelve small islands together with several tiny islands. The Great Nicobar is the largest of all the islands.

The Ganga

Ganga is the longest river of India. The total length of the Ganga river from its source to its mouth (measured along the Hughli) is 2,525 km of which 1,450 km is in the Uttar Pradesh, 445 km in Bihar and 520 km in West Bengal. The remaining 110 km stretch of the Ganga forms the boundary between Uttar Pradesh and Bihar.

The Ganga originates as Bhagirathi from the Gangotri glacier in Uttar Kashi District. It is joined by the Alaknanda at Devaprayag and the combined flow of the Bhagirathi and the Alaknanda is known as Ganga. After traveling 280 km from its source, Ganga enters plains at Haridwar. At Allahabad, about 770 km south-east of Haridwar, Ganga is joined by Yamuna, which is its most important tributary. After Farraka in West Bengal, the river ceases to be known as the Ganga. It bifurcates itself into Bhagirathi-Hughli in West Bengal and Padma-Meghna in Bangladesh. After traversing 220 km further down in Bangladesh, the Brahmaputra joins it at Goalundo and after meeting Meghna 100 km downstream the Ganga joins the Bay of Bengal.

Northernmost Point Of India

Northernmost point of India is disputed. The Siachen glacier in the state of Jammu and Kashmir is the northern most point under Indian control. India claims the entire state of Jammu and Kashmir on the basis of Instrument of Accession signed in 1947, which inter alia includes Gilgit, Baltistan, and Kanjut. Gilgit, Baltistan, and Kanjut are presently under the control of Pakistan. The northern most point, if we take the whole state of Jammu and Kashmir in consideration, is Dafdar in the Taghdumbash Pamir near Beyik Pass in Kanjut.

SMALLEST STATE IN INDIA

Goa with an area of 3702 sq. km is the smallest state in India. Goa was a Portuguese colony and was liberated from Portuguese rule on December 19th, 1961. After its independence, Goa along with Daman and Diu was accorded the status of Union Territory. On May 30th, 1987, the Union Territory was split, and Goa was elevated as India's twenty-fifth state, with Daman and Diu remaining Union Territories. Goa is one of the most developed states of India. Tourism is the mainstay of Goa. Panaji is its capital and Vasco, its largest town. The main language of Goa is Konkani.

SOUTHERNMOST POINT OF INDIA

Indira Point, the southernmost tip of the Great Nicobar island is also the southernmost point of land in the territory of India. It is at 6° 45' N latitude. Indira Point was formerly known as Pygmalion Point and it was named so by the late Rajiv Gandhi after his mother on a visit to the Andaman and Nicobar Islands. A large part of the Indira Point was submerged under the sea due to the tsunami generated by the 2004 Indian Ocean earthquake. The sea is now slowly retreating back to its original position. Indira Point is also a favourite nesting site for exotic sea animals.

The Tortoise: Westermost Point Of India

Kutch-During the monsoon season the region becomes virtually an island resembling a tortoise or a 'Katchua', surrounded by seawater. West of Ghuar Mota in Gujarat is the westernmost point of India. Its Latitude/Longitide is 23.67 N/ 68.52 E. Ghuar Mota is in the Kutch region of Gujarat. Other cities located near Ghuar Mota are: Koteshwar, Mudia, Panadra, Pipar, Ber Mota, Ber, Lakhpat, and Lakhpal.

Kutch was one of the princely states of India during the British rule. It has an extreme climate and the temperature ranges from 20° C in winter to 45° C in summers.

State With Least Number Of Districts In India

Goa is the state with least number of districts in India. It has two districts: North Goa and South Goa.

The North Goa district has an area of 1736 sq. km. The geographical position of Goa is marked by 15° 48' 00" N to 14° 53' 54" N latitudes and 73° E to 75° E longitudes. North Goa shares its boundaries with the Sawantwadi and Dodamarg, of Ratnagiri District and Kolhapur District of Maharastra state and South Goa District shares with it the southern boundary.

South Goa is situated between the latitudinal parallels of 15° 29' 32" N and 14° 53' 57" N, and longitudinal parallels of 73° 46' 21" E and 74° 20' 11" E. Arabian Sea is to the west of district. North Goa district is to the North and Uttar Kannada district of Karnataka in the East and South. The total geographical area of the district is 1966 sq km.

Drass: Coldest Place In India

Drass in western Ladakh is the coldest place in India. It is also the second coldest place in the world after Siberia. Temperatures drop down to about -40 degrees Celsius in winters. However, summers in Drass are balmy and many trekkers and campers visit Drass during the summer time. Drass has an altitude of 3230 m and lies 60 km west of Kargil on the road to Srinagar. The Drass valley starts from the base of the Zojila pass, the Himalayan gateway to Ladakh. Drass is a convenient base camp for treks to Suru valley. Inhabitants of Drass are of Dard descent, an Indo-Aryan race believed to have originally migrated to Ladakh from Central Asia.

Largest Alluvial Plain Of The World

The Great Plain of North India also known as Indo-Gangetic-Brahmaputra Plain is the largest alluvial plain of the world. This plain extends for a length of 3,200 km from the mouth of the Indus to that of the Ganga. The plain lies partly in Pakistan and partly in India. The length of the plain in India is around 2,400 km. The average width of the plain varies from 150 to 300 km. It is widest in the west where it stretches for about 500 km. Its width decreases in the east. It is about 280 km wide near Allahabad and 160 km near Rajmahal Hills. The plain widens to about 460 km in Bengal but narrows down in Assam where it is only 60-100 km wide. The plain covers a total area of 7.8 lakh sq km. The northern boundary of the plain is well defined by the foothills of the Shiwaliks but its southern boundary is a wavy irregular line along the northern edge of the Peninsular India.

Largest District In India

Kachchh (also spelled as Kutch) in Gujarat, with an area of 45,652 sq km is the largest district in India. The administrative headquarter of Kachchh is in Bhuj. The district's five main towns are Gandhidham, Bhuj, Anjaar, Mandavi, and Mundra. There are 966 smaller villages in the area.

Kachchh literally means something which intermittently becomes wet and dry. Rann of Kachchh, a significant region of Kachchh district is shallow wet-land which submerges in water during the rainy season and becomes dry during other seasons. Kachchhi and

Gujarati are the dominant languages of the area. Kachchhi draws heavily from its neighboring language groups: Sindhi, Punjabi, and Gujarati.

LARGEST PHYSIOGRAPHIC UNIT OF INDIA

India is divided into five physiographic divisions. These are:

- The Himalayan Mountains
- The Great Plains of North India
- The Peninsular Plateau
- The Coastal Plains
- The Islands

Among these five physiographic units, the Peninsular Plateau is the largest physiographic unit of India. The entire plateau measures about 1,600 km in the north-south and 1,400 km in east-west direction. It covers a total area of about 16 lakh sq km which is about half of the total land area of the country. The Peninsular Plateau is roughly triangular in shape with base coinciding with the southern edge of the great plain of North India and its apex is formed by Kanyakumari in the southern extremity.

LARGEST STATE IN INDIA

Rajasthan with an area of 342,239 sq km is the largest state in India. Before the formation of Chattisgarh as a separate state in the year 2000, Madhya Pradesh was the largest Indian state in terms of area. Rajasthan is located in the western part of India and has two distinct geographical regions with desert on one side and thick forest on the other. Aravalli, the oldest mountain chain, is the dividing line between the two climatic zones of the state. Western Rajasthan encompasses most of the area of the Great Indian Desert (also known as Thar Desert). The eastern region of the state has thick vegetations of Sal, Axlewood, Dhak, and Mesquite.

LENGTH OF COASTLINE OF INDIA

Length of coastline of India, including those of Andaman and Nicobar Islands in the Bay of Bengal and Lakshwadweep Islands in the Arabian Sea, is 7,517 km. Length of coastline of Indian mainland is 6,100 km. Coastline of Indian mainland is surrounded by Arabian Sea in the west, Bay of Bengal in the east, and Indian Ocean in the south. The long coast line of India is dotted with several major ports 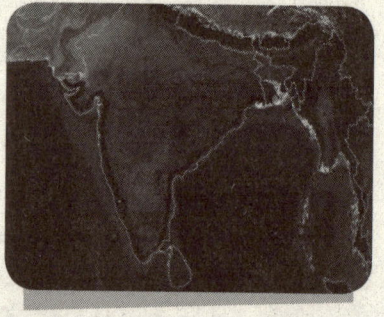 such as Kandla, Mumbai, Navasheva, Mangalore, Cochin, Chennai, Tuticorin, Vishakapatnam, and Paradip. For the effective defence of the Indian coastline, a separate force known as Indian Coast Guard was formed on February 1st, 1977.

MAHE: SMALLEST DISTRICT IN INDIA

Mahe is the smallest district in India. It has an area of 9 sq. km. Mahe is geographically located in the state of Kerala, where as administratively it comes under the control of Union

Territory of Pondicherry. Mahe has the official name of Mayyazhi in the local Malayalam language.

Mahe has a population of about 36,000 according to the 2001 census. The population density of the town is 4,091 per sq. km. Males constitute 47 per cent of the population and females 53 per cent. Mahe has an average literacy rate of 85 per cent. Mahe has two members in the Pondicherry Legislative Assembly, representing Mahe and Palloor.

SMALLEST UNION TERRITORY IN INDIA

Lakshadweep with an area of 32 sq km is the smallest Union Territory in India. Lakshadweep islands lie in the Arabian Sea and extend from 8° N to 12° 20' N and 71° 45' E to 74° E. The islands north of 11° N are known as Amindivi Islands while those south of this latitude are called Cannanore Islands. In the extreme south is the Minicoy Island. The Laccadives, Minicoy and Amindivi group of islands were renamed as Lakshadweep in 1973. All the islands are of coral origin. The islands consist of twelve atolls, three reefs and submerged sand banks. Of the twenty-seven islands, only eleven are inhabited.

SOUTHERNMOST POINT OF INDIAN MAINLAND

Named after the Devi Kanya Kumari Temple in the region, Kanyakumari is the southernmost point of Indian Mainland. Kanyakumari, also known as Cape Comorin, is located in the state of Tamil Nadu. Kanyakumari has great geographical significance as it is the confluence of the Arabian Sea, the Indian Ocean and the Bay of Bengal. The place is famous for its spectacular sunrises and sunsets. Kanyakumari has been associated with great men such as Swami Vivekanada and Mahatma Gandhi. Swamy Vivekananda visited Kanyakumari for deep meditation and enlightenment. To commemorate the visit, a monument known as Vivekananda Rock Memorial, has been built which attracts a large number of tourists. Mahatma Gandhi visited Kanyakumari twice in 1925 and 1937.

Wettest Place In India

Cheerapunji The original name for this town was Sohra (so-har-a), which was pronounced 'Churra' by the British. This name eventually evolved into the current name, Cherrapunji. The name 'cherrapunji' which means 'land of oranges' was first used by tourists from other parts of India. Cherrapunji is the wettest place on the earth. The place receives an annual rainfall of over 1200 cm. Cherrapunji is situated at 56 kms from Shillong, the capital of Meghalaya, in one of the heaviest rain-belts in the world. However, off late, a dispute as emerged between Cherrapunji and the neighboring village of Mawsynram for the crown of 'Wettest Place in the World'. Sometimes, it is Cherrapunji which records highest annual rainfall in the world and sometimes it is Mawsynram. However, meteorologists question the genuineness of the data obtained from Mawsynram. Unlike Cherrapunji, there is no meteorological office at Mawsynram.

STATE WITH MAXIMUM NUMBER OF DISTRICTS IN INDIA

Uttar Pradesh is the state with maximum number of districts in India. It has a total of 70 districts. Uttar Pradesh is the most populous and fifth largest state of India. Only five countries of the world—China, the United States, Indonesia, Brazil and India—have populations larger than that of Uttar Pradesh. Kanpur is the largest city of Uttar Pradesh and as per the 2001 census six cities of Uttar Pradesh, namely, Agra, Allahabad, Kanpur, Lucknow, Meerut, and Varanasi have population of over a million.

2 Colours And Symbols

India is a feast of delight for it has within her many hues and colours. It is a country painted with a special brush displaying elan. Each colour has its own significance out here.

Black in India has connotations with lack of desirability, evil, negativity, and inertia. It represents anger and darkness and is associated with the absence of energy, barrenness, and death.

White in India takes on a more sombre connotation. This is the only colour widows are allowed to wear. It is the acceptable colour at funerals and ceremonies that mark death in the family. The principle is that white, as a colour, repels all light and colours and therefore, when a widow wears white, she disconnects herself from the pleasures and luxuries of active and normal participation in society and life around her. White is also widely accepted as the colour of peace and purity and is diametrically opposite to red, the colour of violence and disruption in the southern half of India.

Red is dynamic and constantly breathing fire in the eyes of the beholder. It incites fear and is the colour associated with one of the most revered goddesses in Hindu mythology–Durga. Her fiery image is enhanced by her red tongue and almost red eyes. Red also stands for purity and is the preferred colour for a bride's garment. Red is a symbol in the Indian psyche. The bride is decked in brilliant hues of red to the red tikka (spot on forehead) that she adorns after the wedding as a sign of her commitment. Red also symbolizes fertility and prosperity. It is the colour of the fertile clay that reaps harvests and better lives, and is used widely in prayers and offerings.

Yellow: Turmeric, while being used for cooking in both the north and the south, is also used in ceremonies, in offering prayers and marriages. Yellow symbolizes sanctity and is an essential herbal ingredient applied on the body and face by women in the sub continent. In a country steeped in religious beliefs, the origin of most colours lies in the powers and mythical lives of its gods.

Blue: The colour blue is associated with Lord Krishna, perhaps one of the most favored gods in India.

Green symbolizes a new beginning, harvest, and happiness. It is also the revered colour of Islam, a large religious presence in India. Green symbolizes nature and therefore is a manifestation of God himself.

The colours of India have mesmerized rulers, outsiders and visitors—perhaps more so because of the stories and legends that bind its people, its culture, and its beliefs. The 'rani' pink of mystical Rajasthan, the pastel hues of southern India, the joyous, bright hues of the northern frontier, and the balmy bright colours of the east offer a kaleidoscopic insight into an almost perfect blend of history and modernism.

Festivals

India stands for its incredible culture, spectacular forts and places, great traditions and rituals. This so called 'country of snake charmers and magicians' can boast of a great civilization. Be it the people, lifestyle or the mystical charm—India has always amazed the world with her uniqueness.

India is a land where every detail of life is different, fascinating and stimulating, however familiar it might first appear. It is an extraordinary, awe-inspiring, beautiful, outrageous and often a witty country.

The landscape is a burst of colours, song, drums, trumpets, and elephants in fancy dress. Festivity is the very essence of India, despite all odds. There is a festival for everything, from weddings and elections to the all-important harvest festival and the arrival of the rains; there are festivals even to honor bullocks and snakes. There are Muslim, Sikh, Buddhist and Jain festivals. But the vast plethora of the Hindu gods has the most festivals. Every temple deity has its own special festival. A deity may visit a fellow deity in another temple, take a bath, change her clothes, or collect his wife. It may be a god's wedding ceremony or it may be the celebration of the past triumphs of a Hindu god, as recounted in the epics. Hindu gods have very worldly emotions and Muslim festivals, as well as the big markets and fairs, attract the quality performers of classical and folk dance, music and singing. Some festivals attract pilgrims, itinerant performers and visitors from all over India and may last for even ten days. Only 4 days have festivities on fixed dates. These are the Republic Day (January 26), Mahatma Gandhi's birthday (October 2), Independence Day (August 15) and Christmas (December 25). Hindu religious festivals are calculated according to the lunar calendar, roughly keeping within a four-week span. The final decisions are made annually by pundits for the following year. Muslim festivals move right around the year.

There is the right place for the right festival. For instance, in September-October festival of Dussehra is best seen at Varanasi (Banaras) and Delhi, where it is called Ram Lila; at Kolkata (Calcutta), it is called Durga Puja. Holi is best enjoyed in Rajasthan, Pongal in Tamil Nadu and Muharram in Lucknow.

Diwali

Diwali, the festival of lights is one of the most prominent festivals of Hindus, which is celebrated with great pomp and show. Lavish arrangements are made for the celebration of this Hindu festival. It is also called Deepavali. The festivity has a lot of religious significance for the people of India. It celebrates the triumph of love and friendship over evil and hatred. It spreads light and awareness by overcoming the darkness.

शुभ दीपावली !

Diwali preaches the lesson of strengthening the bondage of love and friendship by breaking the barriers of enmity. Diwali usually falls on the Amavasya, the fifteenth day of the Hindu month of Ashwin. The celebration of Diwali in India takes place with splendid grandeur. The festivity conveys the message of overcoming ignorance that tends to hinder the path of the light of knowledge.

Diwali is one of the favorite festival of Indians, especially kids, who are fond of firecrackers. It is on this day that people dressed up in beautiful, colourful attire; embellish their homes with various kinds of decorative items. Banners of happy Diwali are placed on the main entrance of the house, so as to warmly welcome the guests.

In the evening, Laxmi Puja maybe conducted. Thereafter, people exchange greetings and sweets. They embrace each other and wish each other a Happy Diwali. Kids seek the blessings of the elders.

Houses are decorated with diyas, candles, lamps and colourful lights. In the evening, the sight of the lighted houses becomes a real feast for the eyes, almost displaying a fantasy world. Every year during Diwali, the markets witness an increasing growth in the sale of lights, candles, and fireworks.

There are many interesting legends associated with the origin and history of Diwali. The legends of Diwali or Deepawali festival mainly consist of the stories taken from the religious scriptures of Hindus. One thing that is common to these legends is the fact that, they all end up with the message that good always triumphs over evil.

The festival is also associated with the legend of Rama and Sita. Lord Rama was asked to leave the kingdom of Ayodhya along with his wife Sita and younger brother Lakshman by his father Dashratha, who was the king of Ayodhya. Lord Rama returned home after the completion of fourteen years of his exile. Lord Rama defeated Ravana, the demon of Lanka and protected the people from the clutches of this evil mind. When he came back home after his victory, he was warmly welcomed by the people of Ayodhya. The day was observed as an occasion for celebrating the victory of Rama over Ravana, thus the triumph of truth over evil.

Then there is the legend of King Bali and Vamana Avatar. The story revolves around the king named Bali, who was very generous. Once it happened that some of the deities went to meet Lord Vishnu and requested him to keep a track of the king's power. On the request of several Gods, Lord Vishnu visited earth, disguised in the form of a dwarf priest named Vamana. The dwarf met the King and said that he is the ruler of the three distinctive worlds, namely, the Earth, sky and the world lying underneath the skies. Vamana asked him to give him the space that he can cover in three steps. The king laughed thinking that a dwarf would hardly be able to cover any space and he agreed to his request. It was at that point of time that the dwarf got converted into Vishnu and his three paces covered the entire earth, sky and the universe. As a result, the king was given the portion of the world lying underneath the skies.

There follows another legend of Narkasur and Lord Krishna. The story is about Lord Krishna, the eighth incarnation of Lord Vishnu, who succeeded in defeating the demon Narkasur. Narkasur had brought about havoc, creating fear in the minds of people. He would kidnap pretty women and forcefully make them live with him. Lord Vishnu heard the cries of the victims and appeared in the form of Lord Krishna and fought with the devil Narkasur, and finally succeeded in freeing the women from the clutches of the monster Narkasur. It is a great story that

speaks of the triumph of good over evil.

There is also the legend of Krishna and the mountain. Long back in the village of Gokula, it happened that people offered prayers to Lord Indra, who was believed to send the rains and make the crops grow. It was at that time that Lord Krishna came and asked people to pray the mountain Govardhan, as the mountain as well as the land surrounding it was quite fertile. This made the God Indra angry and he brought a thunderstorm. This incident terrified the people and they went to Krishna for help. Then Lord Krishna lifted the mountain with his one finger, giving a sigh of relief to the people of Gokula village. It also paved way for the growing of crops. This incident reminds the Hindus to thank God for the bounty of nature.

During Diwali, the markets are stocked with various decorative items, ranging from attractive banners and door hangings to ornamental candles, diyas and lamps. When people talk about Diwali, the festival of lights, the first thing that strikes the mind is undoubtedly the Diwali decorations.

They begin with the task of embellishing their houses for Diwali and turning it brighter; the first and foremost thing is to clean the house thoroughly, so that it is completely clean. People usually apply a fresh coat of paint on their walls and doors to lend a revitalizing look to their dwelling place. Diwali is the time to adorn your house in a traditional manner, using the various decorations for the festival.

Most people try to change the basic settings of the furnishings and other decoration pieces. It give the houses an entirely different look.

They adorn the houses with traditional door hangings, which are beautified with mirror work. As a part of Diwali decorations, people draw rangolis that are very pleasing to look at. If you want to further enhance the appeal of rangoli, you can border it with decorative diyas and candles. They illuminate the entire house with colourful lights.

On the festivity of Diwali, people gather to offer prayers to Goddess Lakshmi and Lord Ganesha who are believed to bring good health, wealth and prosperity. There is a proper time for performing the Diwali puja. People keep their doors and windows open at the time of Diwali Lakshmi puja, thus giving a welcome to the deities. It is believed that the deities visit the homes on the occasion of Diwali.

At the time of Diwali puja, people make offerings to the Agni Devta, the Lord of fire. It is a way of offering the food, specially prepared on the Diwali festivity, to the deities. Diwali puja basically consists of sixteen steps, in which each step represents a ceremony that should be performed by a Hindu during his lifetime like Diwali Puja welcoming the deities, providing them a place to sit, washing their feet, offering food and clothing to them and seeking their divine blessings.

The offerings also include fresh scented flowers and various kinds of herbs. The other things associated with the Deepawali Lakshmi Ganesh pujan are singing of songs, chanting, ringing of bells and blowing of conch shells. To ward off the evil spirits, tiny lamps made from clay, more commonly known as diyas, are lit. It also serves as a means of expressing self-enlightenment.

After the puja is over, sweets are offered to the Goddess as 'Naivedya'. It is then distributed in the form of 'Prasad' to the people. It is followed by the exchanging of gifts and greeting cards. People visit their friends and relatives to wish them Happy Diwali. Some of the delicacies during this festival are Badam Doodh-Basic Ice Cream Recipe, Besan Ladoo, Dahi Wada (Lentil Fritters in Yogurt sauce), Gajar Ka Halwa, Gur Ke Chawal (Rice with Jaggery), Malpua, Moong Daal Halwa, Sitaphal Rabdi and Meethi Kachori.

There are many interesting legends associated with the origin and history of Diwali. The legends of Deepawali festival mainly consist of the stories picked from the religious scriptures of Hindus. One thing that's common to these legends is that, they all end up with the message that good always triumphs over evil.

Durga Puja

Durga puja is a festivity that can be dated back to the ancient times. Numerous references have been made about Durga puja celebrations in Indian literature from the 12th century onwards. The traditions remain unchanged, but the style of celebration has undergone major transformation. In the past, it was considered to be a festivity of the rich and powerful people.

With the local clubs, the festival celebration has become cosmopolitan in nature. In the contemporary times, Durga puja is like a grand extravaganza. Many days before the arrival of this festivity, people are full of excitement and enthusiasm. As a part of Durga puja celebrations, beautiful pandals are erected and embellished with flowers. Conchshells and drums have a major role to play in setting the mood for festivity celebration.

There is a pandal in almost all localities. With the migration of

Bengalis to other parts of the country, Durga puja is now celebrated in other parts of the country also. For the craftsmen and artisans, Durga puja is the time for displaying their creativity and also earning their livelihoods. The first four days of Durga puja are very hectic and witness lot of activities like different kinds of competitions are held to energize the people. The artists get a platform to show their talent to the people and make a name for themselves.

The main celebration takes place from the sixth day, i.e. more commonly known as maha shashthi. On this day, the priest displays the deity while performing the puja. Women usually fast on this day praying for the well-being of their families. They break their fast in the evening time with fruits and luchis (different kind of bread made from flour). A visit to the local pandal is like a must.

On the seventh day, i.e. maha saptami, people wake up early and on an empty stomach, they offer prayers to the deity. After the prayers are over, Prasad is offered to the deity. During the lunch time, special meal is served to all those, who congregate in the pandals. If you visit the pandals during the evenings, the view is very pleasing, as people with glowing faces are dressed in colourful clothes. The dazzling clothes and ornaments, spectacular lighting, beating of drums set the mood for celebrations.

The eighth day, which is known as maha ashtami, is one of the most significant days of the Durga puja festivity. While chanting the shlokas, the priest performs a special puja known as the sandhi puja. On this day, the reflection of the deity is seen in a bowl of water. This gives a feeling of the movement of deity. The puja is popularly known as pranpratishtha (means breathing life into the idol). By the evening, merry making is at its peak.

Pandal to pandal visit is the favorite pastime activity during the occasion of Durga puja. On the ninth day that is known as maha navami, meat is served in most of the pandals as a part of bhog. Since, it is the penultimate day of the festival celebration, people start realizing that the festivity is about to get over. This is how the Durga puja celebration takes place in India.

Durga puja is a festivity that takes place with great pomp and show in Bengal. Though, it is celebrated in almost all the places of West Bengal, but the celebrations are especially lavish in Kolkata (Calcutta). There are a couple of ancestral houses in Kolkata that have been serving as the main venue for Durga puja celebrations for the many past decades.

Durga puja in Kolkata, India is not just an occasion for sharing joyous moments, but also has a lot of religious significance for its people. When it's time for Durga puja celebrations, each and every locality of Kolkata begins preparations with fervour. Kolkata starts making special arrangements. Beautiful pandals are set up and adorned with lights. The beautiful images of Goddess Durga are displayed in the pandals. After the performance of special pujas, various cultural programs are held. There are a number of activities to entertain people, like folk music and dance performances.

The shopping malls are flooded with people, who buy different decorative items for their household. Women buy jewelry and ethnic clothes. People spend like anything when it comes to Durga puja festivity. Kolkata is abuzz with activities during Durga puja. The city turns into a hub of life. Everybody is busy shopping in the markets. There is a festive touch in the air throughout. Festivities in Kolkata without Durga Puja would be like Christmas without Santa Claus.

Goddess Durga is believed to be the mother of the universe and the power behind the work of creation, preservation, and destruction of the world. Since time immemorial she has been worshipped as the supreme power of the Supreme Being and mentioned in many scriptures - Yajur Veda, Vajasaneyi Samhita and Taittareya Brahman.

The word 'Durga' in Sanskrit means a fort, or a place which is difficult to overrun. Another meaning of 'Durga' is 'Durgatinashini', which literally translates into 'the one who eliminates sufferings'. Thus, Hindus believe that goddess Durga protects her devotees from the evils of the world and at the same time removes their miseries.

There are many incarnations of Durga: Kali, Bhagvati, Bhavani, Ambika, Lalita, Gauri, Kandalini, Java, Rajeswari, etc. Durga incarnated as the united power of all divine beings, who offered her the required physical attributes and weapons to kill the demon 'Mahishasur'. Her nine appellations are Skondamata, Kusumanda, Shailaputri, Kaalratri, Brahmacharini, Maha Gauri, Katyayani, Chandraghanta and Siddhidatri.

Goddess Durga is depicted with eight or ten hands. These represent eight quadrants or ten directions in Hinduism. This suggests that she protects devotees from all directions.

Like Shiva, Mother Durga is also referred to as 'Triyambake' meaning the three-eyed Goddess. The left eye represents desire (the moon), the right eye represents action (the sun), and the central eye knowledge (fire).

She sits on a lion, which represents power, will, and determination. Mother Durga riding the lion symbolizes her mastery over all these qualities. This suggests to the devotee that one has to possess all these qualities to get over the demon of ego.

Durga has many weapons. The conch shell in Durga's hand symbolizes the 'Pranava' or the mystic word 'Om', which indicates her holding on to God in the form of sound. The bow and arrows represent energy. By holding both the bow and arrows in one hand 'Mother Durga' indicates her control over both aspects of energy—potential and kinetic. The thunderbolt signifies firmness. The devotee of Durga must be firm like thunderbolt in one's convictions. Like the thunderbolt that can break anything against which it strikes, without being affected itself, the devotee needs to attack a challenge without losing his confidence. The lotus in Durga's hand is not in full bloom, it symbolizes certainty of success but not finality. The lotus in Sanskrit is called 'pankaja' which means born of mud. Thus, lotus stands for the continuous evolution of the spiritual quality of devotees amidst the worldly mud of lust and greed. The 'Sudarshan-Chakra' or beautiful discus, which spins around the index finger of the Goddess, while not touching it, signifies that the entire world is subservient to the will of Durga and at her command. She uses this unfailing weapon to destroy evil and produce an environment conducive to the growth of righteousness. The sword that Durga holds in one of her hands symbolizes knowledge, which has the sharpness of a sword. Knowledge which is free from all doubts, is symbolized by the shine of the sword. Durga's trident or 'trishul' is a symbol of three qualities - Satwa (inactivity), Rajas (activity) and

Tamas (non-activity)—and she is remover of all the three types of miseries - physical, mental and spiritual.

Devi Durga stands on a lion in a fearless pose of 'Abhay Mudra', signifying assurance of freedom from fear. The universal mother seems to be saying to all her devotees: 'Surrender all actions and duties onto me and I shall release thee from all fears.'

Goddess Durga represents the unification of all the divine forces to overpower the evil spirits. To fight with the demon Mahishasur, the gods decided to create a really powerful force. At that moment, lightening came forth from the mouths of the three Hindu Gods, namely Brahma, Vishnu and Mahesh, giving rise to a gorgeous woman with ten hands. The deities supplied her with their weapons, thus giving her all the powers of the universe.

According to the epic *Ramayana*, Lord Ram performed the chandi puja, so as to seek the divine blessings of Goddess Durga. He did so for killing Ravana, the devil king of Lanka who had kidnapped his wife Sita. Goddess Durga secretly told him that he can kill Ravana. In the war between Rama and Ravana, Lord Rama succeeded in defeating the devil and returned to his kingdom along with his wife Sita and younger brother Lakshman.

According to the great Indian epic *Mahabharta*, the Pandavas wandered in the forests for a long period of twelve years. They kept their weapons on a Shami tree before leaving for the court of king Virat, where they spent their last one year in disguise. On the completion of that one year, which happened on the day of Vijayadashmi, i.e. Dussehra, they brought down the weapons that they had kept on the Shami tree. On this day, they came forward and revealed their true identity. Since then, this day is celebrated as Vijaydashmi or Dusshera and involves the exchange of Shami leaves as a symbol of victory and goodness.

Kumbh Mela

Kumbh Mela is a mega event that is organized four times in every twelve years in India. The festivity has truly come into the limelight and acquired fame not just in India, but made its presence felt even globally. The celebration of Kumbh Mela takes places at four different places, namely Prayag (Allahabad), Ujjain, Haridwar and Nasik. Maha Kumbh Mela, also known as the great Kumbh Mela, is held only once in twelve years in Allahabad.

Millions of devotees come from all across the country to witness this distinguished festivity. The credit for initiating the Kumbh Mela festivity can be attributed to the King Harshvardhana. Kumbh Mela of Ujjain, took it as an opportunity to make donations to help the poor and needy and to strengthen the faith of people of all religions in the divine power.

Kumbh Mela has a lot of significance for people in India, as it gives them an opportunity to liberate themselves from the sufferings and wash away all their sins. Kumbh Mela is believed to have the largest congregation of ascetics, yogis, sadhus, sages and common men living on the planet Earth.

Kumbh Mela is not just a mere festivity like Diwali and Holi, but holds lot of importance for people in India. People look up to Kumbh Mela with highest regard, as this event gives them a golden opportunity to liberate themselves from the miseries and sufferings of life. It enables them to take a holy dip in the sacred water and wash away all the sins they have committed in the past.

Prayag is the point where the three holy rivers Yamuna, Ganga and Saraswati meet, which is more often referred to as Triveni Sangam. This is the spot where Kumbh Mela is conducted. Devotees congregate here and perform several rites and rituals. A number of ceremonies are performed, out of which the most important is the bathing ceremony that takes place on the banks of the rivers in each town.

Pilgrims come here and take holy bath and thus get rid of their sins. Out of all the rituals, the most important is the bathing ceremony, which is performed on the auspicious dates as calculated on the basis of astronomy.

Ardh Kumbh and Maha Kumbh Mela are often interspersed with each other, but there is indeed a difference between the two. Ardh Kumbh Mela is celebrated once in every six years after the Maha Kumbh Mela, the celebration of which takes place every twelve years. The venue keeps on changing from time to time.

Maha Kumbh Mela, also known as the great Kumbh Mela, is conducted in every three years at each of the four distinct locations, namely Prayag (Allahabad), Ujjain, Nasik and Haridwar. The next Maha Kumbh Mela is held at each destination on the completion of twelve years. Ardh mela on the other hand takes place six years after Maha Kumbh Mela at each of these locations.

Kumbh Mela is believed to have the largest congregation of ascetics, yogis, sadhus, sages and common men living on the planet Earth. People from all across the country assemble here to observe this famous mela.

There are many interesting legends about the origin and celebration of the Kumbh Mela. The story revolves around the fight between demons and Gods for the nectar of immortality. The origin of Kumbh Mela can be traced back to the Vedic period, when the deities and demons arrived at a consensus to work together in the task of churning 'amrit', i.e. the nectar of immorality from the Ksheera Sagara (the primeval ocean of milk). It was decided that the nectar would be shared amongst all on an equal basis.

When the Kumbh or the pitcher full of amrit appeared, the demons played truant and they escaped the place with the nectar. The Gods also followed them and fought with demons in the sky for acquiring the pitcher of amrit. The battle went on for twelve consecutive days and nights, which was equivalent to twelve human years. It is said that during the war, a few drops of amrit fell on the earth at four distinctive spots, namely Prayag, Haridwar, Ujjain and Nasik. These are those four points or locations, where Kumbh Mela festival is celebrated four times in every twelve years.

Kumbh Mela Bathing ceremony takes place at the following destinations:

At Prayag near the city of Ahmedabad, where the three holy rivers namely Ganga, Yamuna and Saraswati meet.

At Haridwar that lies in the state of Uttar Pradesh, from where river Ganga enters into the plains from the Himalayas.

At Nasik in the state of Maharashtra on the banks of river Godavari.

At Ujjain in the state of Madhya Pradesh on the banks of river Ksipra.

During the Maha Kumbh Mela, the devotees bask in the nectar or amrit. Here 'amrit' refers to the light of knowledge that will awaken your inner conscience and pave way for attaining enlightenment.

Rig Veda mentions the significance of convergence of rivers Ganges, Yamuna and Saraswati at Prayag or Sangam. References can be found about the significance of this ritual in Varaha Purana and Matsya Purana as well. There is a belief that the ashram of the learned Bharadvaja, where Lord Ram, Laxman and Sita lived at the time of their exile, was situated at Sangam. It is said that a number of saints including the great Shankaracharya and Chaitanya Mahaprabhu visited Sangam and observed the Kumbh Mela. The great Indian

epics such the *Ramayana* and *Mahabharata* have mentioned that a yagna was conducted by Lord Brahma at Sangam.

Onam

The celebration of the grand Onam festivity continues for a long period of ten days in Kerala. However, in some small regions, it is restricted to only four to five days. It is believed that the celebrations used to take place for a month and that too in a very lavishly.

People still believe in their traditional values and the essence of celebration is unchanged. They give due importance to the customs and rituals of the bygone times and follow them religiously. The celebrations cover a period of ten days.

Day 1: Atham

It marks the beginning of the celebration of Onam. It is considered to be a very auspicious day by Keralites. On this day, people start preparing the pookalams, which is one of the main highlights of this occasion.

Day 2: Chithira

The second day is known as Chithira. On this day, no special rituals are performed but people visit temples to seek God's blessings.

Day 3: Chodhi

The third day is called the Chothi. This day witnesses a number of activities. The markets get overcrowded, as people get engrossed with the task of buying new apparels, accessories and various decorative household items.

Day 4: Visakam

Like the third day, the fourth one also is hectic.

Day 5: Anizham

The major highlight of the fifth day of Onam celebration is the boat race. The boat race is one of the most favourite sporty activity that is more popularly known as Vallamkali.

Day 6: Thriketa

By the sixth day, which is known as Thriketa, people who have migrated to other places start visiting their homes to celebrate Onam with their family.

Day 7: Moolam

By the seventh day, the entire nation is excited and passionate about the grand extravaganza.

Day 8: Pooradam

The eighth day bears a lot of significance for Keralites. Worshippers prepare idols of deities with clay.

Day 9: Uthradam

On the ninth day, people start making special arrangements for welcoming the spirit of King Mahabali. From this day onwards, the entire nation gets involved in a full-fledged manner in of Onam celebrations.

Day 10: Thiruvonam

The tenth day is known as Thiruvonam. This is the main day of Onam. The entire nation, especially the state of Kerala is abuzz with activities on this day.

Pongal

'Pongal' literally means 'boiling over'. Pongal usually takes place on the 15th of January. For Tamils, it is one of the most prominent festivals. The entire South India gets actively involved in its preparations. The chilly weather serves like a messenger for the people of South India, as it intimates them about the arrival of Pongal.

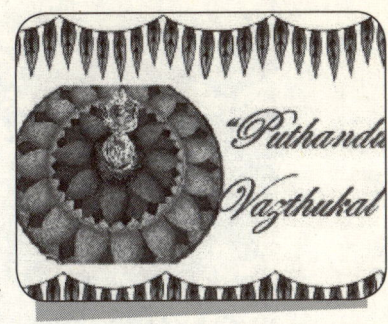

The festivity spans over a period of four consecutive days. It starts with Bogi Pongal and ends with Kaanum Pongal, which is also known as the Thiruvalluvar Day. This occasion has a lot of significance, especially for farmers, who put their hearts and souls in the sowing and harvesting of crops. Pongal celebrations observe the end of the harvesting season.

During Pongal, markets are flooded with various kinds of farm produces. Amongst the Hindus, it is celebrated as a thanksgiving festival, in which people offer their sincere thanks to the Hindu Gods for showering their blessings on them.

- On the first day, which is more popularly known as Bogi Pongal, people thank Lord Indra, the God of heaven.
- The second day is dedicated to Lord Surya.
- The third day is meant for thanking the cattle.

Day 3- Mattu pongal is a day of thanking the cows and buffaloes, as they have a major role to play in harvesting crops. Had they not been there, it wouldn't have been possible to plough the lands. The third day witnesses the hosting of a violent bull taming contest that is more commonly referred to as Jallikattu.

- The fourth day, which is known as Kaanum Pongal, marks the end of Pongal. On this day, people go shopping, visit their friends and relatives, exchange greetings and wish each other 'Happy Pongal'. People visit local temples and seek divine blessings. The entire nation swings, sings and dances to the tunes of music.

Pongal celebrations continue for four consecutive days. The festival usually falls in the month of Shravan. It is basically a harvest festival that is celebrated with fervor and gaiety by the people in the Southern states of India. Pongal witnesses a lot of activities. In fact, entire South India comes alive, when it's the time for Pongal celebrations.

The origin and history of Pongal can be dated back to the times of Sangam Age i.e. from 200 B.C. to 300 A.D. The Sanskrit Puranas also contain mentions of Pongal. Initially Pongal was celebrated as a Dravidian Harvest festival.

People observed 'Pavai Nonbu', as part of Pongal. It is one of the most prominent festive occasions that took place during the rule of Pallavas. Celebrated in the Tamil month of Margazhi, this festivity was initiated by young girls who offered prayers to the God for sending rain, thereby paving way for bringing prosperity for people.

Throughout the month of this festivity, they did not consume milk or any milk products. They did not oil their hair during this period. All these traditions have led to the celebration of the Pongal, as we know today.

Legends of Pongal festival:

Lord Shiva's story-Once it happened that, Lord Shiva asked his bull named Basava to visit the earth and meet the human beings. He was asked to convey the message that, the humans must take an oil massage and bath on a daily basis and as far as eating is concerned, they can

eat only once in a month. By mistake, the bull wrongly conveyed to the people that, they must eat every day and as far as oil massage and bathing is concerned, it must be done only once in a month. This act of Basana made Lord Shiva very furious. As a result, Lord Shiva punished him to live on the earth forever and help people in ploughing fields and growing more food.

Lord Indra's story-Once it happened that, Lord Krishna in the days of his childhood, decided to teach Lord Indra a lesson, as he had become a bit too arrogant after becoming the king of all deities. Lord

Krishna went to meet the cowherds and told them to stop worshipping Lord Indra. This enraged Lord Indra and he brought about a major thunderstorm along with rains that continued for three consecutive days. Seeing this calamity, people went to Lord Krishna with cries of help.

Then, Lord Krishna lifted the mountain Govardhan, and that too with a single finger. This incident made Lord Indra realize his mistake.

Celebration time: In the epic of *Mahabharata*, it was mentioned that the gopis (milkmaids) used to draw Kolams to lessen their pain of Krishna's absence. The art of Kolam-making is practiced in almost all the states but known by different names like Alpana in Bengal, Mandana in Rajasthan, Muggulu in Andhra Pradesh, Puvidal in Kerala, Rangoli in Maharashtra and Karnataka, and Sanjhi in Uttar Pradesh.

Kolam is not just an aesthetic art, but a means of expressing happiness and prosperity. The rice flour finds its way in the making of Kolam patterns for Pongal. The bright red colour that is used to border the Kolam is believed to ward off the evil spirits. On Pongal, the entire family gets engrossed with the task of making Pongal kolam designs. A kolam may be simplistic or intricate in patterns.

Rakhi

Rakhi is a festivity that celebrates the beautiful relationship between a brother and sister. It is a very sacred relation that truly deserves a special celebration. It is owing to this reason that, Rakhi festival celebration is given so much importance in India. It is one of the most prominent festivities, which is celebrated with gaiety and enthusiasm by Indians.

The rituals and customs have undergone major transformation along with the style of celebrations today.

People shop for new apparels, rakhis, diyas and other gifts for their siblings. Gifts appear in lucrative packaging and this is what tempts people into buying them. Assorted chocolates are always in demand. The sweet shops and confectionary shops witness maximum business during the festive occasion.

On Raksha bandhan, people get up early and wear their new attire. The day begins with offering prayers to deities. After seeking God's blessings, sisters bring their thali and perform the aarti. Thereafter, they apply tika on the foreheads of their brothers by mixing rice and vermillion. Then they tie rakhi on the wrists of their brothers.

They offer sweets and pray for their brothers' good health and prosperity. The brother then presents her a gift and vows that he will protect her till the last breath of his life and promises to stand by her side in her good and bad times. This is how Rakhi festivity is celebrated in India.

Rakhi is celebrated in the holy month of Shravan. The origin and history of Rakhi can be dated back to the mythological times. Most Indian epics have mentioned this festivity. There are many interesting legends associated with the history of the festival.

There is an interesting legend related to the war between the demons and Gods. This story has been mentioned in the Bhavishya Puran. In the war between the devils and the Gods, the Gods were on the verge of defeat. Once it happened that, Lord Indra who was leading the Gods, went to meet Guru Brihaspati for finding a solution to this problematic situation. The Guru asked Lord Indra to tie a pure thread on his wrist that was powered by the holy mantras chanted on the Shravan Purnima. The queen of Lord Indra, who is more often referred to as Indrani, empowered the thread with the sacred mantras and then tied it on his wrist on the decided day. It was the power of the sacred thread known as Raksha that helped in protecting the Gods from the clutches of the evils and paved way for their victory. Since then, the tradition of tying a thread has continued on as a gesture of concern.

Then there is the story of Bali. King Bali was a great worshipper of Lord Vishnu. Seeing his devotion, Lord Vishnu decided to protect his kingdom. He even left his abode that was located in Vaikunth. It was Goddess Lakshmi's desire to be with him in his abode at Vaikunth. Disguised as a Brahmin woman, Goddess Lakshmi went to meet King Bali and asked him, if she could take refuge till her husband returns. During the celebration of Shravana Purnima, Lakshmi tied a sacred thread on the King's wrist. When the king enquired, she revealed her identity and her purpose of visiting him. The king was touched by her concern for Lord Vishnu. Seeing this, he requested Lord Vishnu to accompany her. It is due to the extreme devotion of King Bali towards Lord Vishnu that, the festivity is sometimes also known  as Baleva. Since then, the tradition of calling upon the sisters on the occasion of Raksha Bandhan for the thread-tying ceremony started. It is also believed that the tradition of Raksha Bandhan was followed by Yama, the Lord of death and his dear sister named Yamuna. There are some popular kinds of Rakhis:

Sandalwood rakhi: These rakhis are made with sandalwood. To lend an ethnic look to the Rakhi, sandalwood beads are extensively used.

Cartoon rakhi: The most favorite cartoon characters that are finding their way in the designing of rakhis include Donald Duck, Mickey Mouse, Mogli, and now Doreamon.

Musical rakhi: These rakhis are loved by young kids.

Floral rakhi: Owing to their natural fragrance, floral rakhis are very much in demand.

Zari rakhi: Owing to their shine, the silver and golden zari rakhis are increasingly popular.

Resham rakhi: Beautiful and soft are what best describe the Resham rakhis.

Beads rakhi: These rakhis are very much in fashion.

Mouli: It is a simple red colour thread that is extensively used as a part of Hindu religion customs and rituals. It is also known as kalava.

Holi - Festival Of Colours

Holi is a lively Hindu fiesta. Holi celebrates the spirit of life which is happiness and merriment. The backdrop to this festival is the liveliness of spring at its peak, when colours and flowers bloom across the courtyards and streets throughout the country.

The excitement is best seen in youngsters, who go around the streets in groups and have fun with colours. Colour spray, traditional dances and, delicious food and sweets are the main attractions of Holi. Linked to Radha-Krishna, Holi is also observed by worshipping and other rituals. Indeed Holi is the festival of colours, merriment and happiness.

On the first day of Holi or the full moon day, coloured powder known as 'gulal' is arranged on a 'thali' (platter) and coloured water is kept in a small brass pot known as 'lota'. As a good omen, the eldest male member of the family sprinkles colours from the 'thali' and 'lota' on each member of the family. People light huge bonfires at community grounds to commemorate the burning of Holika and the new life granted to the child-devotee Prahlad. As the fire burns brighter, people perform folk songs and play drums on rhythmic beats around the bonfires, asking for blessings of the holy fire. In some areas, people offer the first fruits, coconuts, and harvest to the holy fire.

The embers of this fire are then carried home and people light fire in their houses from them. On the next day, children, men and women form separate groups and visit each other's houses smearing each other's faces and bodies with 'aabir' and 'gulal', and spurting coloured water on people using 'pichkaris' and water balloons. The young pay respects to their elders by sprinkling some colours on their feet.

Women decorate their homes with flowers and traditional 'rangolis' made on the doorways with coloured rice powder or flowers and offer sweets, snacks and 'thandai', a milk-based cool drink to all those who visit their houses.

Holi marks the end of winter and the beginning of spring. The festival breathes an air of romance and social merriment. Celebrated predominantly in northern India, generally 'hasya kavi sammelan' or humor poem-get-togethers are arranged. This is India's way of observing April Fool's Day. Traditionally, natural colours are prepared at home from flowers, especially from Tesu and Palash.

There are many legends associated with this festival. There was a mighty demon king named Hirnakashyipu who had won all the three worlds of heaven, earth and hell and had thus reached his hubris. He had assumed that he could defeat even Lord Vishnu with his valor. He went to the

extent that he had enforced a law that everybody would worship him instead of gods and deities. However, his little son Prahlad refused to accept his commands and continued to worship Lord Vishnu with complete devotion. Infuriated by this defiance of his son, he ordered his soldiers to throw him down a hill. Praying fervently and having full faith in Lord Vishnu, Prahlad did not retract from his word. True to his faith, Lord Vishnu rescued him at the last moment.

Hirnakashyipu invoked the help of his sister Holika, who had a boon that she could walk through the fire unharmed. The wicked aunt agreed to the evil desires of her brother and entered the fire with her nephew Prahlad. However, the brother and sister had forgotten that Holika could only enter the fire alone or she would perish. Thus, blessed by Lord Vishnu, the child Prahlad remained unharmed but Holika got burnt and died instantly. Holi is thus celebrated to commemorate the death of the evil aunt, after whom the festival is named, and the new life granted to Prahlad for his devotion and faith. To this day, cow dung is hurled into the fire and obscenities are shouted at the Holi fire at some places to insult Holika.

Another story is applied to this festival also. During the reign of Prithu, there was a terrible ogress called Dhundhi, who loved to devour innocent children. She had performed severe penances and had won several boons from the deities that made her almost invincible.  However, due to a curse of Lord Shiva, she was not so immune to the pranks and abuses of young boys as she was to weapons and arrows. One day, the courageous boys of the village decided to get rid of her and chase her away from the village forever. They got intoxicated and drunk on bhaang, and then followed Dhundi to the limits of the village, beating drums, making loud noises, shouting obscenities and hurling insults at her. They continued until she left the village for good. This is the reason that even today young boys are allowed to indulge themselves in rowdiness, using rude words and intoxication on Holi.

Then there is the love play of Radha and Krishna. Lord Krishna has often been portrayed as a naughty prankster in his childhood and a loverboy in his youth. His beloved Radha and the cowherd girls or 'Gopis' in general, loved him even more for his pranks and eve teasing. The

Holi of Braj is famous all over India for its intimate connection with the divine deities and their love plays. It is said that when Krishna was a young boy, he asked the reason for his dark colour while Radha was so fair. His mother Yashoda playfully suggested that he should smear

colour on Radha's face too and change her complexion to any colour he wanted. Captivated by the idea, Krishna proceeded to do so and thus, introduced the play of colours on Holi. Even today, Holi is one of the most important festivals of Braj, where the men of Nandgaon and women of Barsana play 'latthmar Holi' in remembrance of the playful throw of colours by Krishna on 'Gopis' and their resistance. The trace of eroticism and romance pervades Holi as depicted in the love plays of Krishna and Radha. In Mathura, Vrindavan, Gokul and Barsana, Holi is a two-week long festival featuring play of colours, folk songs called 'Hori', folk dances such as 'Raas-Lila', and staging various aspects of Radha and Krishna's love.

Then there is the legend of the sacrifice of Kamadeva. According to Hindu mythology, the world is looked after by the Trinity of Gods - Lord Brahma, the creator; Lord Vishnu, the nurturer; and Lord Shiva, the destroyer. According to a legend, Goddess Sati, the daughter of Daksha Prajapati, one of the first sons of Lord Brahma, married Lord Shiva against the wishes of her father. Thus, Daksha did not invite her and her husband to a grand yagna arranged by him. When Sati came to know about the event in her father's house,

she thought it to be a slip of mind and proceeded to participate in the event despite the warnings of her husband. But once she reached there, she realized her fault and was infuriated by her husband's insult. As penance for her disobedience, she entered the fire. When Lord Shiva came to know of her sudden demise, he was furious. Even after he had controlled his anger, he started a severe meditation and renounced all work. The world's balance soon crumbled in his absence and Sati took rebirth as Goddess Parvati to try and win Lord Shiva's heart and wake him up from his trance. She tried all ways to get Shiva's attention. When she had exhausted all her feminine ways, she invoked the help of Kamadeva, the Indian cupid-god, who agreed to help her in the cause of the world despite the risks involved. He shot his love-arrow into Shiva's heart. Disturbed in his trance, Lord Shiva opened his third eye that fired anger and instantly incinerated Kamadeva. It is said that it was on the day of Holi that Kamadeva had sacrificed himself for the good of all beings. Later, when Lord Shiva realized his mistake, he granted Kamadeva immortality in invisible form. To this day, people offer sandalwood paste to Kamadeva to relieve from his stinging burns, and mango blossoms that he loved on Holi.

Symbols

Namaste: This word has been derived from two Sanskrit words 'nama' meaning to bow and 'te' meaning you. It is a beautiful way of greeting people in India. Namaste is wished by folding the palms together resembling the prayer position.

Namaste is a gesture of saying that 'I honour the spirit in you which is also in me.' It is a way of expressing that you and I are equal. While saying Namaste, the folded hands are usually kept close to the heart, thus indicating that I am glad to meet you and I am saying this from heart. It is usually accompanied by slight bowing of head. It also acts as a mark of respect for elders. Namaste has a lot of significance for the people of India. The hands that are held in unison represent the meeting of spirits.

Namaste is a gesture that is used in various contexts, on one hand where it is used for greeting the elders, then on the other hand, it is brought to use in the practice of yoga as an important mudra. It is widely used in the culture of Buddhists.

Om: Om is of utmost importance in the Hindu religion. The symbol Om is considered to be very sacred, as it represents the Brahman, i.e. the source of life. For Hindus the day begins with the chanting of Aum Mantra. Many Hindus wear pendants of Om, as it is very auspicious. The Om symbol signifies divinity and the oneness of all the creations of God. Om or Aum presents the never ending Brahman, where all forms of life exist. When you take a deep breath and chant Om, it leads to calming effect, which will totally relax your mind and body. It is the first stage of meditation and aims at drawing your attention away from all other tensions that have occupied your

mind. All that you need to do is to hide in a peaceful place, sit down on the floor, gently close your eyes, take a deep breath and chant Om. While doing so, completely relax your muscles. Don't tighten your muscles; otherwise you won't be able to feel the energizing effect of chanting Om.

Gayatri mantra:

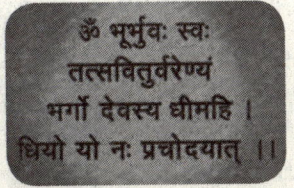

Aum Bhoor Bhuwah Swaha,
Tat Savitur Varenyam
Bhargo Devasaya Dheemahi
Dhiyo Yo Naha Prachodayat

A large part of population chants Gayatri mantra every day in the morning. It is the primary mantra in Hinduism. People believe that chanting the Gayathri mantra raises the intellectual level of the person who performs it. Known as the mother of the Vedas, Gayatri mantra opens the gateway for wisdom, thereby teaching people to follow the righteous path and perform good deeds. In the devotion of Goddess Gayatri, the Gayatri mantra is chanted three times in a day.

Numerous references have been made about the Gayatri mantra in the Upanishads. Each and every word of the mantra has an important message to convey, which if followed sincerely, can make your life beautiful and peaceful. Based on truth, it preaches people to follow the path of honesty and always indulge in activities that are meant for the goodness of mankind. Gayatri mantra is considered to be the best means for connecting to God.

Rishis and Munis chose the words for the Gayatri mantra and arranged them in such a manner that, the chanting of this mantra created a powerful force. Gayatri mantra has a lot of significance. While chanting the mantra, one must always close one's eyes and try to concentrate on each and every word that is said and then is seen the magical effects.

Moksha: Moksha is a term that refers to liberation from the cycle of death and rebirth. Every person must strive hard and perform good deeds, so that his soul may rest in peace after his death. A person, who attains Moksha, gets freedom from all sorts of sufferings and pain. When a person gives away the materialist pleasures of life and gets involved in

social activities to serve mankind, he heads his way towards heaven. Moksha is a very broad term which encompasses numerous aspects like peace, knowledge and enlightenment.

In Hindu religion, self-realization is considered to be the best means to achieve Moksha. The Hindu Dharma preaches the path of Karma and Bhakti. Well, there can be different ways of achieving salvation. In totality, there are four paths of attaining liberation from the cycle of death and rebirth, namely, selfless work, self dissolving love, deep meditation, and total discernment.

In Hindu religion, Moksha is associated with the concept of self-realization, in which an individual understands the purpose why he is being sent on earth. When a person realizes the power of God and understands his ultimate goal, he strives hard to reach his final destination, i.e. Moksha or salvation. Among Hindus, Moksha is viewed as the unification of man and God.

Swastika: Swastika symbol has a lot of relevance for people in India. Though, the sign is adopted by people of all religions, but it is especially popular amongst the Hindus. The term Swastika has been derived from the Sanskrit word 'Svastika', which means well-being. Swastika is considered to be a mark of auspiciousness and good fortune. Red Swastika is the sign of Hindus, which depicts a

cross with four arms of equal lengths. The end of each of the arms is bent at a right angle. At times, dots are also added between the arms.

Indo Aryans, Greeks, Hittites and Celts extensively used the Swastika cross in historic times. Swastika has been a sacred symbol of Hindus since ages. The symbol is considered to be highly auspicious and thus it is quite often used in the art and architecture of Hindus. It finds a special place for itself in wedding decorations. Swastika designs can be found in temples, doorways, clothing, cars etc. Most wedding cards have the Swastika symbol imprinted on them.

Swastika is a symbol of good fortune in Buddhist religion. It represents the footprints and heart of Buddha. Thus, it is considered to be very holy and was extensively brought to use by Buddhists. In fact, in all the images of Gautam Buddha, we find the Swastika cross imprinted on his chest, palms and feet.

Swastika symbol has much more relevance and significance in the Jain religion as compared to the Hindu religion. In Jainism, Swastika represents the Seventh Jina, more popularly known as the Tirthankara Suparsva. It is one of the most prominent auspicious symbols of the present era. In the cultural traditions of Svetambar Jains, Swastika is one of the main symbols of the ashta-mangalas.

Peepal: Peepal tree is considered highly sacred, as people believe that Lord Vishnu and many other Gods used to reside underneath it. Peepul plant is regarded as the representation of various Hindu Gods and Goddesses. The tree is also believed to be associated with the Mother Goddess during the period of Indus Valley civilization. People revere the peepal tree and also perform a puja in its dedication.

The botanical name of peepal is Ficus religiosa. This holy plant is known by different names in different languages like Bodhi in Sanskrit, Piplo in Gujrati, Al or Aryal in Malayalam etc. It is said that peepal tree protects mankind from the evil eye and also keeps away dreadful dreams. Mentions have been made about the holiness of peepal tree in Vedas. Peepal tree is also known for its medicinal value.

Peepal tree has a lot of reverence and significance for people. People worship the tree and perform a puja. The tree is known for its heart-shaped leaves that have long narrowing tips. The origin of peepal tree can be traced back to the times of Indus Valley Civilization (3000 BC-1700 BC) in the Mohenjodaro city.

Peepal tree is of great medicinal value. Its leaves serve as a wonderful laxative as well as tonic for the body. It is especially useful for patients suffering from jaundice. It helps to control the excessive amount of urine released during jaundice. The leaves of peepal are highly effective in treating heart disorders. It helps to control the palpitation of heart and thereby combat the cardiac weakness.

Rudraksha: Rudraksha is a term that is used to refer to the broad leaved evergreen trees that can be commonly found in the areas

lying between the Gangetic plains and the foothills of the Himalayas. When fully ripe, a thin blue coloured outer shell covers the seeds of rudraksha. It is owing to this reason that, sometimes the rudraksha seeds are also known as blueberry beads. The rudraksha beads have a lot of significance. Rudraksha is a popular traditional Indian medicine that is extensively used to treat several kinds of diseases.

A person who wears rudraksha gets all his sins washed and heads towards his ultimate destination. The devotees of Lord Shiva are usually given rudraksha for peace. A person tends to become pure after wearing rudraksha beads.

The term rudraksha refers to the tears of Lord Shiva. Lord Shiva meditated for several years for the well-being of all creatures. But, when he opened his eyes to see around, he saw people in pain. Rudraksha beads are basically the tears of Lord Shiva that rolled down his eyes after seeing the sufferings of people. It is owing to this reason that these rudraksha beads are considered to be of paramount importance. In the eyes of people, rudraksha beads are the gift of God to mankind. There are various types of rudraksha beads available, each having its own importance.

Tilak: The forehead mark tilak has a lot of significance in India, as it is believed to be associated with good luck. Tilak is applied on the space between the eyebrows, which is referred to as Ajna Chakra. Tilak is applied on the point at which the third eye or the spiritual eye is believed to open.

The Hindu symbol tilak stands for victory, success and good fortune. The tradition of applying tilak is being practised since ages. There are different kinds of tilak; some are made with sandal paste, while others use kumkum, sacred ashes (vibhuti) and turmeric. In many Hindu families, tilak is worn on a daily basis, before stepping out of house to ensure health and safety. Other people wear it on specific religious occasions.

The worshippers of Lord Shiva, called Saivites, apply tilak made of sacred ashes, since it symbolizes purity, consecration and sanctification.

Tulsi: Tulsi is a consecrated plant that holds lot of importance for traditional Hindus. In most Hindu homes, people worship tulsi plant on a daily basis. Many people keep the plant in front of their house, since it has a lot of reverence for them.

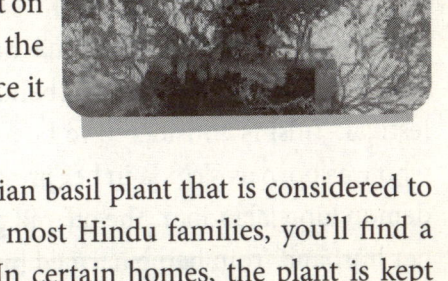

Tulsi is the most prominent Indian basil plant that is considered to be very sacred. In the house of most Hindu families, you'll find a tulsi planted in the courtyard. In certain homes, the plant is kept in a specially constructed structure and is surrounded by images of Hindu Gods and Goddesses from all four sides.

The Indian herbal plant tulsi has a lot of significance in the Hindu religion. The term 'tulsi' is used in the context of one who is absolutely incomparable. Tulsi has a lot of reverence for the Hindus. In fact, people worship tulsi every day in the morning as well as in the evening. This Indian basil basically grows in warm and tropical regions. There are two main varieties of this aromatic plant, namely Shyama tulsi and Rama tulsi. Out of the two, the former one is of greater medicinal value. Rama tulsi, on the hand, is primarily used for worship.

Tulsi plant has a lot of significance for mankind, due to its manifold medicinal benefits. Tulsi leaves are widely used in the preparation of Ayurvedic medicines. It is known to promote the longevity of life.

The extracts obtained from the plant are extensively used for curing various diseases such as common cold, inflammation, malaria, heart disease, headaches etc.

Tulsi is considered to be highly sacred in Hindu religion. Most Hindus offer daily prayers to Tulsi Devi. There are many interesting legends about tulsi. There is a famous legend about Krishna Tulsi, which suggests that tulsi was the incarnation of a gopi, who was deeply in love with Lord Krishna. She was cursed by Radha, the consort of the Lord.

Tulsi vivah is a grand festivity that has a lot of significance for Hindus. There is an interesting legend behind the celebration of Tulsi vivah festival. Tulsi is considered to be an incarnation of Maha Lakshmi, who was born as Vrinda in her previous birth. Tulsi was married to a demon king Jalandhar. She offered prayers to Lord Vishnu to protect her husband from being harmed by any God.

Chyawanprash: This is a wonderful Ayurvedic health tonic, which is increasingly gaining popularity in India. It is an ancient Ayurvedic tonic that serves as the best and the most natural health supplement for the human body. Chyawanprash is a brown coloured sticky paste that is quite thick in consistency. It has a blend of sweet and sour taste and this is what makes it quite popular amongst youngsters.

It boosts energy levels and strengthens the body's immune system. Chyawanprash is believed to be truly an elixir of life, as it helps prolong the longevity of life. Known for its nutritional value, it is highly beneficial for the human body and also helps to get rid of various forms of diseases.

Chyawanprash is spelled differently by people. Some call it chyavanprash or chyavanaprasha, while others pronounce it as chyavanaprasam and chyawanaprash. The credit for the initial preparation of this herbal tonic can be accredited to Chyawan Rishi. In fact, this tonic has been named after him.

Chyawanprash is a reservoir of benefits. There are distinct ways of defining Chyavanprash such as energy booster, rejuvenator, health tonic and many more. It offers a multitude of health benefits for which it has become so popular in India. In today's times, people are leading such unhealthy lifestyles that is characterized by improper diets, lack of exercise and sedentary jobs.

A large number of companies are engaged in the manufacturing of Chyawanprash, therefore the composition differs from one brand to another. The herbs that are brought to use varies from twenty-five to eighty in number, however, one ingredient that remains unchanged is amla. In fact, it is one of the prime herbs used for preparing Chyavanprash. Other vital ingredients consist of cinnamon, honey, asparagus, dried catkins, ghee, dehydrated sugar cane etc.

Karma: The term Karma refers to the deeds performed by an individual, which ultimately decides his destiny. Thus, karma and destiny are associated with each other. The kind of karma that a person carries out tells a lot about his character and personality. A person is not born great or small, it is his deeds or the karmas that make him noble or criminal. God maintains an account of our karmas and accordingly we receive the fruit, which can be good or bad.

There are basically three types of Karmas:

Sukarma: It refers to the good deeds or the positive actions that a man performs for the goodness and welfare of mankind. It is an act, in which both the parties, as in the one who is performing the act and the one for whom the deed is carried out, both derive pleasure and happiness. It is based on the concept that if I do something for you, you feel thrilled and seeing you happy and cheerful, I will derive pleasure and contentment.

Vikarma: It refers to the selfish acts that are performed to cause harm to others or to pose hindrances in the success and prosperity of others. Well, these kinds of karmas are usually performed by those who can't see others happy and their joy lies in the sorrows of others.

Akarma: It refers to neutral actions. It means the activities that you are carrying out neither cause any kind of harm to the other person nor do they bring any sort of happiness to others.

The law of karma is based on the concept of cause and effect relationship. It says that, every action has an equal and opposite reaction. The kind of deeds an individual performs, determines his fate. Karmas are performed only in human life. Karmas ultimately decide if a person, after death, will head for heaven or hell.

The law of karma instead emphasizes that it is not your luck that gives you happiness or suffering, but your own karmas decide your destiny.

3 Dimensions

Taj Mahal

The Taj Mahal is the majestic specimen of Mughal architecture that has beckoned tourists from all over the world with its opulence and the innate tale of Emperor Shah Jahan's undying love for his beloved queen. While awestruck tourists have marveled at the extravagance all around, poets and  literateurs have eulogized the Taj as the 'Eternal Monument of Love.'

Apart from eloquent panegyrics, the Taj Mahal has long been regarded as one of the Seven Wonders of the World alongside famous structures such as the Great Wall of China and the Pyramids of Egypt. The Taj Mahal is one of the frontrunners in an ongoing global campaign launched to officially select the new Seven Wonders of the World.

Today the Taj Mahal has metamorphosed into one of the prominent icons associated with India. A flourishing tourism industry has come up in Agra that relies heavily on the allure of the Taj. In addition to the hordes of regulation tourists, the Taj Mahal also figures prominently in the itinerary of visiting dignitaries and statesman.

The architecture of the Taj is unique. The finest and the most spectacular edifice of the Mughal era, the architecture of Taj Mahal imbibes myriad elements of Hindu, Persian and earlier Mughal architecture. This white marble mausoleum is indeed the cynosure of all eyes. The sprawling complex of Taj Mahal comprises a main gateway, an elaborate garden, a mosque (to the left), a guest house (to the right), and several other palatial buildings.

The Taj Mahal is steeped in rich history and captivating legends. With its opulent structure and romantic connotations, the Taj Mahal has spawned a wealth of facts and information that often astound the uninitiated.

The Taj Mahal's history is essentially the tale of an emperor's undying love for his beloved queen. This magnificent edifice was erected by Mughal Emperor Shah Jahan as a mausoleum for his queen Mumtaz Mahal. Shah Jahan was the fifth ruler of the powerful Mughal dynasty which held sway over vast swathes of India between sixteenth and nineteenth centuries.

The Taj Mahal is located in the historic city of Agra in the north Indian state of Uttar Pradesh. The location of Taj Mahal on the banks of river Yamuna makes for an enchanting spectacle. The city of Agra was established in 1475 by Badal Singh and after a brief period of rule by the Lodhi dynasty, it eventually fell to the Mughal invaders led by Babur.

An edifice of massive proportions, the Taj Mahal is unrivaled for its majestic grandeur and sheer opulence. The culmination of over twenty-two years of painstaking craftsmanship, this monument of love is a masterpiece representing artistic virtuosity at its best.

AJANTA ELLORA

The Ajanta Ellora caves are fine specimens of ancient rock-cut cave temples. Located in the Aurangabad district of Maharashtra, the Ajanta Ellora caves are UNESCO-designated World Heritage Sites. Even though Ajanta and Ellora are often mentioned in the same breath, the cave temple clusters in these locations are different from each other in many aspects.

While the caves in Ajanta are primarily Hinayana and Mahayana Buddhist caves, the Ellora cave temples belong to Hindu, Buddhist and Jain religions. There are variations in the architectural and sculptural dimensions as well. In comparison to the Ajanta caves which are embellished with profuse, intricate paintings and sculptures, the Ellora caves are mundane, drawing inspiration from the Vajrayana school of Buddhism.

The Ajanta caves remained hidden from public knowledge until a unit of British soldiers from the Madras Army stumbled upon them in 1819 during a hunting expedition. In contrast, the Ellora caves, due to their location on the ancient north-south trade route or the dakshinapatha, had served as a refuge for traders, priests and pilgrims who plied the route to the western ports. In fact, the Kailash was used for worship until the 19th century.

The rock-cut Ajanta caves are renowned masterpieces for their unique architecture and the profusion of sculptures and paintings. The walls and ceilings of the Ajanta caves are chiseled with exquisite carvings and paintings that chronicle the life of Lord Buddha.

The Ajanta caves are treasure troves of exquisite paintings that depict scenes from Jataka tales and the life of Lord Buddha. Beautiful murals adorning the walls, ceilings and the pillars bear testimony to the versatility of ancient artistes.

Set amidst the sylvan landscape, the Ajanta caves are ancient Buddhist caves hewn out of basalt rock formations. These caves are located at the Lenapur village in the Aurangabad district of Maharashtra state.

The Ellora caves represent a unique synthesis of Buddhist, Jain and Hindu cave temples, all scooped out of the vertical face of the Charanandri hills. Located in the Velur village of the Aurangabad district in Maharashtra, the Ellora cave complex is home to 34 cave temples and monasteries.

The crown jewel among the Ellora caves, the Kailash temple, epitomizes the zenith of ancient rock-cut architecture. Also known as the Cave 16, the Kailash temple is an awe-inspiring edifice with its massive proportions and exquisite carvings.

Iron Pillar

The Iron Pillar in Delhi is an intriguing piece of architecture well-known for its astonishing resistance to corrosion for over 1600 years. Located at the center of the Quwwat-ul-Islam mosque, the Iron Pillar is the solitary Hindu relic in the sprawling Qutub complex constructed by Qutb-ud-din Aibak after plundering the existing Hindu temples. The Brahmi inscriptions engraved in the pillar credits Gupta king Chandragupta II Vikramaditya (375 AD-414 AD) with the construction of the Iron Pillar.

The Iron Pillar, 7.5 meter tall and weighing approximately 6.5 tonnes, is made up of ninety-eight per cent wrought iron of pure quality. The Iron Pillar of Delhi is considered a tribute to Lord Vishnu, the patron deity of the Gupta kings and it is believed that once a figure of Garuda, the carrier-bird of Vishnu, crowned the capital of this slender pillar. The inscriptions mention that the pillar was originally located at a place called Vishnupadagiri and historians have identified this place as modern-day Udayagiri.

How the Iron Pillar was later relocated to Delhi remains a question shrouded in mystery. Even the amazing rust-resilient nature of the pillar had been a baffling riddle for archeologists and metallurgists.

The celebrated Iron Pillar of Delhi is widely regarded as an architectural wonder for the way it has defied rust through the last 1600 years. The Iron Pillar has long been an enigma for metallurgists who have been unable to unravel the reason behind this stubborn resistance to corrosion. Made of ninety-eight per cent of wrought iron, this tall, sleek pillar is bonafide proof of the mastery Indian ironsmiths had achieved in the extraction and processing of iron.

Sarnath Lion Capital

The Sarnath Lion Capital is a major and significant sculpture because of its adaptation as the national emblem of India. It has also been considered as the Lion Capital of Ashoka after Maurya king Ashoka who reigned in the northern part of India during the 3rd century BCE. The Lion Capital originally crowned the Ashoka pillar at Sarnath, one of the many pillars erected by Ashoka to propagate the tenets of Buddhism.

Ashoka built the Sarnath pillar to commemorate the site of the first preaching of Lord Buddha, where he taught the Dharma to five monks. Even though the pillar is still in its original location, the Ashoka Lion Capital has been shifted to the Sarnath Museum for better preservation. The Lion Capital of Ashoka comprises four lions, standing back to back, mounted on a cylindrical abacus. The abacus features the sculptures of an elephant, a galloping horse, a bull, and a lion, separated by intervening twenty-four-spoked Dharma wheels over a bell-shaped lotus.

The Sarnath Lion Capital is replete with symbolism inspired by Lord Buddha's life. The four animals in the Sarnath capital are believed to symbolize different phases in Lord Buddha's life. The elephant is a representation of Queen Maya's conception of Buddha when she saw a white elephant entering her womb in a dream. The bull represents desire during the life of the Buddha as a prince. The horse symbolizes Buddha's departure from palatial life while the lion represents the attainment of Nirvana by Lord Buddha.

The National Emblem of India is an adapted version of the Lion Capital of Ashoka at Sarnath. The Government of India adopted the emblem on January 26, 1950.

Buland Darwaza

Buland Darwaza is the highest gateway in India. This was built by the Mughal Emperor Akbar in 1601 A.D. at Fatehpur Sikri to commemorate his victory over Gujarat. Buland Darwaza is 53.63 m high and 35 meters wide. The structure is approached by forty-two steps.

Buland Darwaza is made of red and buff sandstone, decorated by carving and inlaying of white and black marble. The Buland Darwaza is semi-octagonal in plan and is topped by pillars and chhatris. It is adorned with calligraphic inscriptions from the Quran. There are thirteen smaller dome kiosks on the roof, stylized battlement and small turrets and inlay work of white and black marble. An inscription on the central face of the Buland Darwaza displays Akbar's religious broad mindedness. It is attributed to Jesus Christ and reads, 'The World is but a bridge, pass over but build no houses on it.' A Persian inscription on eastern archway of the Buland Darwaza records Akbar's conquest over Deccan in 1601 A.D.

LARGEST DOME IN INDIA

Gol Gumbaz, situated in Bijapur district of Karnataka, is the largest dome in India. Gol Gumbaz has a diameter of 124 feet and is the second largest dome in the world, next only to St. Peter's Basilica in Rome. The dome was built by Muhammad Adil Shah in the year 1656. It has a floor area of 1700 m² and a height of 51 m. The walls of the structure are 3 m. thick. The dome contains tombs of Muhammad Adil Shah, his two wives, mistress, daughter, and grandson. Gol Gumbaz is an architectural wonder as it stands unsupported by pillars. The most remarkable feature of Gol Gumbaz is its acoustical system. Even the faintest whisper around the dome echoes several times.

Largest Monastery in India

Tawang Monastery in Arunachal Pradesh is the largest monastery in India. The monastery is 3 storeys high and occupies an area of 140 sq m. It is enclosed by a 610 m long compound wall. Within the complex there are sixty-five residential buildings and ten other structures.

Tawang Monastery is one of the most largest monasteries of Mahayana sect in Asia. It was founded by the Mera Lama Lodre Gyasto in 17th century AD in accordance to the wishes of the 5th Dalai Lama, Nagwang Lobsang Gyatso. The monastery is also known in Tibetan as Galden Namgey Lhatse, which means a true name within a celestial paradise in a clear night. The library of the monastery has valuable old scriptures—mainly Kanjur and Tanjur, numbering 850 bundles.

Largest Temple Corridor in India

The corridor of Ramnathswamy Temple at Rameshwaram is the largest temple corridor in India. The temple has 1220 metres of magnificent corridors and has 1200 gigantic granite columns. Ramnathswamy temple was built in the 17th century. The temple is situated close to the sea on the eastern side of the island and has a 54 metre tall gopuram.

Rameshwaram is an island situated in the Gulf of Mannar at the tip of the Indian peninsula. It is one of the twelve Jyotirlingas of India. It is an important pilgrimage destination for Hindus. According to the Hindu mythology, Lord Rama performed thanksgiving rituals at Rameshwaram after his triumph over the demon king Ravana. Therefore, Rameshwaram attracts Vaishnavites and Saivites.

Tallest Statue in India

The statue of Gomateshwara at Sravanbelagola in Karnataka is the tallest statue in India. The statue is 17 metres (55 ft) high and is visible from a distance of 30 km. The gigantic monolithic statue is carved out of a single block of granite and stands majestically on top of a hill. This statue of Lord Gomateshwara was created around 983 AD by Chamundraya, a minister of the Ganga King, Rajamalla. Lord Gomateshwara was a Jain saint, hence the place is an important Jain pilgrimage center. The statue of Gomateswara shows the recluse completely nude, in the Jain custom. The neighboring areas have Jain bastis and several images of the Jain Thirthankaras. At Sravanbelgola the Mahamastakabhishekam festival is held once in twelve years, when the image of Gomateswara is bathed in milk, curd, ghee, saffron, and gold coins.

The statue of Sardar Vallabhbhai Patel in Gujarat will be the tallest statue in the world with an 182 metres tall installed near the giant Narmada Dam or also known as the Sardar Sarovar Dam.

Largest Cave in India

Amarnath Cave in Jammu and Kashmir is the largest cave in India. The width of the cave is around 40 yards, its height is about 75 feet; and the cave slopes 80 feet deep down inside the mountain. Amarnath Cave is an important pilgrimage shrine for the Hindus. The cave is famous for the image of Shiva, in the form of a lingam that is formed naturally of an ice-stalagmite, and which waxes and wanes with the moon.

Amarnath Cave is situated at an altitude of 3888 m and is 45 km from Pahalgam. The trek from Pahalgam to Amarnath Cave is on an ancient peregrine route. The 45-km distance is covered in four days, with night halts at Chandanwari, Sheshnag, and Panchtarni.

Largest Church in India

Se Cathedral in old Goa is the largest church in India. The original building was constructed of mud, stones, and straw and was erected in 1510. It was dedicated to St. catherine. In 1538 the church status was elevated to that of a cathedral with the establishment of the  Diocese of Goa. The cathedral as it stands today took ninety years to be completed. The Portuguese viceroy, Dom Francisco Coutinho, the Count of Redondo (1561-1564) commissioned its construction. Work on the building began in 1562 and was completed in 1652. The height of Se Cathedral's front piece including the cross is 115 2/3 feet and its breadth is 100 4/3 feet. The total length of the cathedral is 250 feet and it breadth id 181 1/3 feet. Externally, Se Cathedral is built in half Tuscan and half Doric style, and internally it is built in the Mosaic-Corinthian style.

Largest Gurudwara in India

Golden Temple in Amritsar is the largest Gurudwara in India. In fact, Golden Temple is the largest Gurudwara in the world. Golden Temple is also known as Harminder Sahib and is considered to be the most sacred shrine of Sikhs. Golden Temple was built during the  leadership of the fifth guru, Guru Arjan Dev (1581-1606). The temple construction was started in 1588 and was completed in 1601.

Golden Temple is surrounded by a small pond of water, known as the Sarovar which consists of Amrit (Holy Water). The temple has four entrances, signifying the importance of acceptance and openness. All devotees are expected to cover their heads as a sign of respect and wash their feet in the small pool of water as they enter the Golden Temple.

Largest Mosque in India

Jama Masjid in New Delhi, overlooking Chandni Chowk and the Red Fort, is the largest mosque in India. The mosque was built by Mughal emperor Shahjahan in 1656. It has typical Mughal architecture with three gateways, four towers and two minarets. The Jama Masjid is made up of red sandstone and white marble. About 25,000 people can pray here at a time. The mosque has a vast paved rectangular courtyard, which is nearly 75 m by 66 m. The whole of the western chamber is a big hall standing on 260 pillars all carved from Hindu and Jain traditions. The central courtyard is accessible from the east. The eastern entrance leads to another enclosure containing the mausoleum of Sultan Ahmed Shah. It took fifteen years to build the mosque and more than five thousand artisans worked on it.

Oldest Church in India

St Thomas Church at Palyar in Trichur, Kerala is considered to be the oldest church in India. In 52 A.D. Thomas Didaemus, one of the twelve apostles of Jesus Christ is believed to have landed at Musiris (Cranganore) in Kerala. He made his first converts both Jews and Hindus at Palayur a town now in Trichur district, Kerala. There he built a small church with an altar, which he consecrated. The Palayur church still stands at the same site and is the oldest church in India. In the 17th century Reverend Fenichi enclosed the original church with a new outer building, as the wooden walls of the old church had been destroyed with time. But the original altar consecrated by St. Thomas still remains at this site.

4 Icons

Mahatma Gandhi

Gandhi is the 'Father of the Nation' for a country with a billion people. Mahatma Gandhi was born as Mohandas Karamchand Gandhi on October 2, 1869 at Porbandar, located in the present day state of Gujarat. His father Karamchand Gandhi was the Diwan (Prime Minister) of Porbandar. Gandhi's mother Putlibai was a pious lady and under her tutelage Gandhi imbibed various principles of Hinduism at an early age. In 1883, all of thirteen and still in high school, Gandhi was married to Kasturbai as per the prevailing Hindu customs. For a person of such extraordinary visionary zeal and resilience, Mahatma Gandhi was by and large an average student in school and was of a shy disposition. After completing his college education, at his family's insistence, Gandhi left for England on September 4, 1888 to study law at University College, London. During his tenure in London, Mohandas Gandhi strictly observed abstinence from meat and alcohol as per his mother's wishes.

Upon completion of his law degree in 1891, Gandhi returned to India and tried to set up a legal practice but could not achieve any success. In 1893, when an Indian firm in South Africa offered him the post of legal adviser Gandhi was only too happy to oblige and he set sail for South Africa. This decision alone changed his life and with that, the destiny of an entire nation. As he descended in South Africa, Gandhi was left appalled at the rampant racial discrimination against Indians and blacks by the European whites.

After reaching India, Gandhi traveled across the length and breadth of the country to witness personally the atrocities of the British regime. He soon founded the Satyagraha Ashram and successfully employed the principles of Satyagraha in uniting the peasants of Kheda and Champaran against the government. After this victory Gandhi was bestowed the title of Bapu and Mahatma, and his fame spread far and wide.

In 1921, Mahatma Gandhi called for the non-cooperation movement against the British Government with the sole objective of attaining Swaraj or independence for India. Even though the movement achieved roaring success all over the country, the incident of mob violence in Chauri Chaura, Uttar Pradesh forced Gandhi to call off the mass disobedience movement. Consequent to this, Mahatma Gandhi took a hiatus from active politics and instead indulged in social reforms.

The year 1930 saw Gandhi's return to the fore of Indian freedom movement and on March 12th, 1930 he launched the historic Dandi

March to protest against the tax on salt. The Dandi March soon metamorphosed into a huge civil disobedience movement. The Second World War broke out in 1939 and as the British might began to wane, Gandhi called for the Quit India movement on August 8, 1942. Post World War, the Labour Party came to power in England and the new government assured the Indian leadership of imminent independence.

The Mahatma was assassinated by religious zealots but his legacy continues in the concepts he pioneered and in the social reforms he initiated. The bespectacled, Khadi-clad image of Gandhi is indelibly engraved on the conscience of every Indian and on October 2 every year, on the eve of his birth anniversary, a grateful nation pays homage to this frail-bodied man who had the vision and courage to take on the might of the British Empire.

The Cabinet Mission sent by the British government proposed for the bifurcation of India along communal lines which Gandhi vehemently protested. But eventually he had to relent and on the eve of independence thousands lost their lives in communal riots. Gandhi urged for communal harmony and worked tirelessly to promote unity among the Hindus and Muslims. But Mahatma's act of benevolence angered Hindu fundamentalists and on January 13, 1948 he was assassinated by Nathuram Godse.

Over the years, Mahatma's principles of Satyagraha and nonviolence have transcended geographical boundaries and they have been employed by activists elsewhere in the world fighting oppressive regimes. Dr. Martin Luther King Jr. used nonviolent civil disobedience while fighting the Civil Rights Movement for African Americans in the United States. The Nelson Mandela-led African National Congress overthrew the minority white South African government after decades of peaceful non-cooperation movement. Gandhi in letter and spirit still ushers in a vibrant, peaceful world.

Indeed, the Mahatma's ideology has inspired such epoch-making movements in different corners of the world. His love for the homespun khadi has become the style statement of most politicians in India.

Mahatma Gandhi's life is so much entwined with the Indian freedom movement that rarely do people endeavor to acquaint themselves with other facets of his eventful life.

Mahatma Gandhi was born Mohandas Karamchand Gandhi and the title 'Mahatma' was accorded to him much later. Mahatma literally translates to 'great soul' in Sanskrit. Even though opinion is ambivalent as to how Gandhi came to be known as Mahatma, people generally believe that noted poet and philosopher Rabindranath Tagore bestowed the title of 'Mahatma' on Gandhi.

Despite his lifelong pursuit of nonviolence, Gandhi found himself embroiled in a war at an early stage of his life, albeit in a humanitarian role. During his stay in South Africa the Second Boer War broke out and Gandhi organized a voluntary medical unit of independent Indians and indentured laborers called the Indian Ambulance Corps. This unit provided exemplary medical service to wounded black South Africans and post-war Gandhi became a decorated sergeant of the Corps.

Pietermaritzburg in South Africa was the place where Gandhi was thrown out of a train in 1893 after refusing to move from the first class to a third class coach while holding a first class ticket. This unsavory incident proved to be a landmark event in Gandhi's life as he made it a mission to protest such incidents of racial abuse. The downtown of Pietermaritzburg city now hosts a commemorative statue of Mahatma Gandhi.

It is indeed a sad irony that Mahatma Gandhi, the greatest exponent of peace and nonviolence, was never deemed eligible for the Nobel Peace Prize. After four previous nominations, Gandhi was chosen for the Prize in 1948, but because of his unfortunate assassination the Nobel Committee had to shelve their plans and the Peace Prize was not awarded that year.

Time Magazine named Mahatma Gandhi 'Man of the Year' in 1930. In 1999 the magazine declared Mahatma the runner-up to noted scientist Albert Einstein as the 'Person of the Century'.

Mahatma Gandhi fell to an assassin's bullets way back in 1948. But the visions and the philosophy of the Mahatma are as much relevant even today. His teachings and ideology have struck a chord with people from all over the world and many have attempted to portray Mahatma Gandhi's life through different creative avenues. As such one comes across a plethora of examples where the life and the works of the Mahatma have been depicted in popular media platforms such as film, literature, and theater.

The 1982 film, *Gandhi*, is perhaps the most acclaimed tribute to Mahatma Gandhi's life. The film, directed by Richard Attenborough and starring Ben Kingsley as Gandhi, went on to sweep the Academy Awards that year by winning eight Oscars including Best Picture, Best Actor and Best Director. But as far as social impact is concerned, the 2006 Bollywood movie *Lage Raho Munna Bhai* wins hands down for its role in awakening a whole generation of Indian youngsters to the principles of Mahatma Gandhi. The film coined the term Gandhigiri to bring home the relevance of Gandhi's tenets in today's world.

The play 'Mahatma vs. Gandhi' directed by Feroz Khan and starring Naseeruddin Shah as Mahatma, seeks to explore the complex father-son relationship between Mahatma Gandhi and his eldest son Harilal Gandhi. The play 'Me Nathuram Godse Boltoy', directed by Pradeep Dalavi, is an autobiographical take on the life of Mahatma Gandhi's assassin Nathuram Godse. The play generated much controversy for the supposedly unbiased portrayal of the circumstances in which Gandhi's murder was plotted and carried out by Godse.

While films and plays based on Mahatma Gandhi's life are basically serious productions, the same cannot be said about the depictions in television and the Internet. While the MTV cartoon 'Clone High' featured the clone of Gandhi as one of the main characters, the cartoon 'Time Squad' on Cartoon Network has an episode where Gandhi is portrayed as craving for a career in tap dancing, instead of leading the Indian freedom struggle. In the first week of 2007, a video posted in the video-sharing website Youtube.com sparked off a controversy for showing a man dressed as Gandhi gyrating to music and doing a pole dance.

Throughout his life, Mahatma Gandhi held certain principles dear to his heart and unfailingly adhered to them. The Mahatma's words were inspirational tenets of wisdom that inspired an entire nation. He firmly believed and stated, 'Permanent good can never be the outcome of untruth and violence.' He has subtlety of expression: 'First they ignore you, then they laugh at you, then they fight you, then you win.' He was matter of fact in his principles: 'You must be the change you want to see in the world.'

Sri Aurobindo

Aurobindo, known as Sri Aurobindo, (15 August 1872–5 December 1950), born Aurobindo Ghose, was an Indian nationalist, philosopher, yogi, guru, and poet. He joined the Indian movement for independence from British rule, for a while became one of its influential leaders and then became a spiritual reformer, introducing his visions

on human progress and spiritual evolution.

Aurobindo studied for the Indian Civil Service at King's College, Cambridge, England. After returning to India he took up various civil service works under the maharaja of the princely state of Baroda and began to involve himself in politics. He was imprisoned by the British for writing articles against British rule in India. He was released when no evidence was provided. During his stay in the jail he had mystical and spiritual experiences, after which he moved to Pondicherry, leaving politics for spiritual work.

During his stay in Pondicherry, Aurobindo developed a method of spiritual practice he called Integral Yoga. The central theme of his vision was the evolution of human life into a life divine. He believed in spiritual realisation that not only liberated man but transformed his nature, enabling a divine life on earth. In 1926, with the help of his spiritual collaborator, Mirra Alfassa (referred to as 'The Mother'), he founded the Sri Aurobindo Ashram. He died on 5 December 1950 in Pondicherry.

His main literary works are *The Life Divine*, which deals with theoretical aspects of integral yoga; *Synthesis of Yoga*, which deals with practical guidance to integral yoga; and *Savitri*: A Legend and a Symbol, an epic poem which refers to a passage in the *Mahabharata*, where its characters actualise Integral Yoga in their lives. His works also include philosophy, poetry, translations and commentaries on the Vedas, Upanishads and the Bhagavad Gita. He was nominated for the Nobel Prize in Literature in 1943 and for the Nobel Peace Prize in 1950.

The basic objective of his teachings was to increase the level of consciousness of people and make them aware about their true self. His literary works include the writings on varied subjects like the Indian culture, socio-political development of the country, spirituality etc.

When he was seven years old, he was sent to England to complete his education. He did his schooling from St. Paul's School in London and graduation from King's College, Cambridge. Side by side, he learnt several foreign languages like Greek, French, Italian German, Latin, and Spanish. He came back to India when he was twenty-one years old.

At the time of partition of Bengal, during the period between 1905-1912, he led the group of Indian nationalists. Later, he became the editor of a nationalist Bengali newspaper named Vande Mataram.

As time passed by, Sri Aurobindo began losing interest in politics and started concentrating on spirituality. He came across a yogi named Vishnu Bhaskar Lele, who showed him the path of Hindu practice of yoga. He went into the state of deep meditation for a period of four years in Pondicherry. Then, he launched a sixty-four-page monthly review 'Arya'. In the year 1920, his close spiritual collaborator named Mirra Richard joined him. She was more popularly known as 'The Mother'. It is in the companionship of the Mother that Aurobindo Ghosh came up with the idea of establishing an ashram in Auroville.

Sri Aurobindo philosophy is based on the concept of 'reality of being and consciousness' amidst the big universe in which we live. The philosophies of Aurobindo Ghosh were very simple with clarity. He taught people to become aware of their true self and feel the presence of divinity lying within them.

The early writings of Aurobindo Ghosh consist of the poems that he penned down when he was a student in England. He wrote quite a number of plays and poems, during his thirteen years of stay in Baroda.

Founded in the year 1926, Sri Aurobindo ashram has witnessed tremendous growth over the years. From a small group consisting of 124 disciples, today, the Aurobindo ashram has more than 2000 members. The ashram is a very vibrant center that is always abuzz with activities.

Guru Nanak

Guru Nanak, the first Guru of Sikhs, was born to the Bedi family in Nankana Sahib, Punjab on the 20th of October in the year 1469. This great personality was the founder of the Sikh religion. Guru Nanak Dev Ji is revered not just by the Sikhs, but also by the Hindu Punjabis and Sahajdhari Sindhis. The writings that contain the stories related to the Nanak life history are known as the Janamkatha.

People are of the belief that, at the time of birth of Guru Nanak, an astrologer was called upon to prepare his horoscope. The astrologer insisted on meeting him and worshipped Guru Nanak with folded hands. At a young age of five, Nanak began discussing spiritual subjects. When he was seven years old, his father got him enrolled in the nearby school village for pursuing studies. However, very soon, he left the school and started taking private classes.

At the age of thirty, he went missing and people though that, he has drowned in the stream, where he used to go every day for a bath. He came back after three days and started saying that 'There is no Hindu, there is no Muslim'. Since then, he started teaching people and this laid the foundation of Sikhism.

Nanak was married to a woman named Sulakhni, the daughter of a rice trader named Moolchand Chona. They were blessed with two sons. The elder son named Sri Chand turned into an ascetic. On the contrary, the younger son named Lakshmi Das was deeply involved in worldly life. Guru Nanak didn't find his own sons suitable for carrying on the Guruship. He instead handed over this responsibility to one of his favorite disciples named Lehna. Bhai Lehna was later named Guru Angad.

The beliefs and philosophies of Guru Nanak Dev, the first Guru of Sikhs, were not very popular in the beginning. But, today, the teachings of Guru Nanak are ruling the lives of Sikhs. The three teachings of Guru Nanak Dev Ji are known as Nam Simran, Kirt Karo and Wand Chako. The term 'Nam Simran' means think about God. 'Kirt Kaara' preaches people to lead a normal life by earning their living through hard work and honesty. 'Wand Chhako' means to share whatever spare things you have with poor and needy.

The birthday of Gurus is more often referred to as Gurupurab. When it comes to Gurupurab, the birthday of the first Guru of Sikhs, i.e. Guru Nanak Dev is known as the Guru Nanak Jayanti, which is celebrated with gaiety and fervor in India. Guru Nanak Jayanti has a lot of religious significance for Sikhs.

Mahavira

Mahavira and Jain religion are two names that go hand in hand with each other. Mahavir Swami was the last Tirthankara of the Jain religion. Also known as Arihants or Jinas, these Tirthankaras are said to be the Gods of Jains. They are just like any other human being who is born on this earth. But, the difference lies in the fact that, they attain enlightenment through self-realization and meditation.

Lord Mahavira made an incredible contribution in laying down the right code of conduct for Jains. He taught people five main ethical concepts:

- *Nonviolence (Ahimsa)*-he taught his people to follow the path of non-violence and live harmoniously with each other.
- *Non-attachment (Aparigraha)*-he asked people to completely detach themselves from the worldly, materialistic life.
- *Truthfulness (Satya)*-he always preached people to speak the truth and not to deceive anyone.
- *Chastity (Brahmacharya)*-he taught people not to indulge in sensual pleasure.
- *Non-stealing (Asteya)*-he taught people not to keep an eye on other's property.

Mahavir Jayanti has a lot of religious significance for people belonging to the Jain religion. It is observed to celebrate the birthday of the great Lord Mahavira, who was born at Kshatriyakund near modern Patna in Bihar in 599 BC. According to the Gregorian calendar, the Mahavir Jayanti festival falls during the period between March and April. As a part of Mahavir Jayanthi celebrations, Jain temples are beautifully adorned with flags.

The day begins with the performance of a ceremonial bath, in which people bathe the idol of Lord Mahavira. This ceremonial bath is more popularly known as 'abhishek'. The idol of Lord Mahavira is then placed in a cradle and taken for procession. The worshippers congregate in the temple and offer rice, milk, fruits and water to Lord Mahavir.

At various places, lectures are conducted to impart the teachings of Mahavir Swami. The basic idea is to make people understand the real virtues of life. On this day, people spend time meditating and praying to the Lord. People give donations to save cows from getting slaughtered. People come from different parts of the country and throng the ancient temples located at Girnar and Palitana in Gujarat on this festival.

The philosophies of Lord Mahavira are based on the sole purpose of improving the quality of life. The basic idea is to attain spiritual excellence by maintaining ethical behavior and following proper code of conduct. Mahavira philosophy primarily consists of metaphysics and ethics. Metaphysics comprise of three main principles, namely, Anekantavada, Syadvada and Karma. The five ethical principles underlying the philosophy of Lord Mahavira are Satya, Ahimsa, Brahmacharya, Asteya, and Aparigraha.

Lord Mahavira had a strong faith in the theory of Karma and he always said that, it is Karma that decides your destiny. Karma means the deeds that you do, which include both, good as well as bad. The philosophies and teachings of Lord Mahavira are universal truths that are applicable even in the modern world that is plagued by corruption and violence.

He was of the opinion that, in retaliation to anti-social elements, if you start behaving aggressively, you will never be able to find any solution. So, it is always better to come to an amicable solution by following the path of non-violence. Ultimately, it is Ahimsa that paves way for maintaining harmony. So, if you wish to live your life in a peaceful manner and if tranquility is what you are searching for, then adopt the philosophy of the great personality.

Kabir

Kabir Das was the well-known mystic poet, one who brought about a revolution. He was a man of principles and practised what he preached. People called him by different names like Das, Sant, Bhakta etc. As Das, he was referred to as the servant of humanity and thus a servant of divinity.

Kabir played the role of a teacher and social reformer through the medium of his writings, which mainly consisted of the two-line verses called Dohas. He had a strong belief in Vedanta, Sufism, Vaishnavism and Nath sampradaya. He applied the knowledge that he gained through the various experiences of his life. He was always in the pursuit of truth and nothing could hold him back. Kabir was well known for his religious affiliation.

There are plenty of legends associated with the birth and death of Kabir (1440-1518). Some people say that he was born in a Muslim weaver family, while others say that he was born to a Brahmin widow. There is a legend that when he was headed for heaven, a tussle took place between the Hindus and Muslims over performing his last rites. Eventually, in the memory of the great Kabir, his tomb as well as a Samadhi Mandir, both were constructed, which are still standing erect next to each other. According to another legend, in a short span of time before his death, Kabir took a holy bath in the two rivers, namely Ganga and Karmnasha, so as to wash away his sins.

Kabir's poetry is a reflection of his philosophy about life. His writings were mainly based on the concept of reincarnation and Karma. Kabir's philosophy about life was very clear-cut. He believed in living life very simplistically. He had strong faith in the concept of oneness of God. He advocated the notion of *Koi bole Ram Ram Koi Khuda*. The basic idea was to spread the message that whether you chant the name of Hindu God or Muslim belief the fact is that there is only one

God who is the creator of this beautiful world.

Kabir is a well known mystic poet, who is famous for his two line verses that are more popularly known as 'Kabir ke dohe.' Dohas of Kabir expressed love, mysticism and philosophy in the most beautiful manner.

Kabir was against the caste system imposed by the Hindu community and also opposed the idea of worshipping the idols. On the contrary, he advocated the Vedantic concepts of atman. He supported the idea of minimalist living that was advocated by Sufis.

Kabir was strictly against the practice of hypocrisy and didn't like people maintaining double standards. He always preached people to be compassionate towards other living beings and practice true love. He urged the need to have company of good people who adhere to values and principles. Kabir has very beautifully expressed his values and beliefs in his writings that include dohas, poems, Ramainis, Kaharvaas and Shabads.

Mirabai

Mirabai (1498-1547) is a well-known mystic poetess, who had deeply fallen in love with Lord Krishna. Her compositions are widely appreciated in India.

Born at Merta in Nagaur District of Rajasthan, Mirabai is known for her deep love for Krishna. When Mira was six years old, her mother gave her an idol of Krishna, whom she worshipped day and night. At the age of sixteen, her father's elder brother named Viram Deo fixed Mira's marriage with Prince Bhoj Raj, the eldest son of Rana Sanga of Chittor.

Mirabai got married, but she never considered him to be her husband. For her, only Krishna was her husband. She was so much in love with Krishna that, she began neglecting her household duties and thus, she ruined her married life. A few years after her marriage, her husband died but Mirabai refused to commit Sati.

It is believed that when Mira turned thirty, she left the palace and went to Vrindavana in Mathura. She spent most of her time praying to and worshipping Lord Krishna. She kept wandering in search for enlightenment. Finally, she went to Dwarka. She left behind her compositions, which consist of several songs and poems. Her love for Krishna was so deep that, it is said that, she disappeared in the temple of Krishna in Dwarka.

The poems of Mirabai were traditionally known as 'pada', a term that was used in the 14th century to refer to the small spiritual songs. Mirabai composed poems as means to express the deepest feelings of her heart.

Shankaracharya

Shankaracharya, a well-known spiritual leader is also known as Sri Adi Shankaracharya which means 'teacher at the feet of God.' He deserves the entire credit for promoting the principles of Advaita Vedanta. He preached the concept of union of soul, i.e. Atman and Brahman. He traveled to several parts of the country for propagating the Advaita Vedanta philosophy through various discourses and debates.

According to most texts, Adi Shankaracharya (686-718) was born as the son of Namboothiri Brahmin couple, Shivaguru and Ar in a place called Kalady, which is a small village in Kerala, India. It is believed that this great soul survived for only thirty two years. It is said that, Shankaracharya was born after many years of his parents' marriage. His parents had offered prayers to Lord Shiva at the Vadakkunnathan temple for childbirth.

There is an interesting legend associated with the birth of Adi Shankaracharya. It is believed that, Lord Shiva appeared Sankara's parents' dreams and asked them to make a choice, whether they want to have a mediocre child who lives a long life or a gifted child who would not survive for long. They mutually decided to go in for the second option. Later, a son was born to them, who was named Shankara. Shankara is a Sanskrit word, which means bestower of goodness. Adi Shankaracharya lost his father when he was very young. When he was five years old, he began his student life. He always wanted to lead the life of a monastic.

Adi Shankaracharya had strong faith in the philosophy of Advaita Vedanta. Advaita is a term which basically means identity of the self (which is more commonly referred to as Atman) and the whole (Brahman). Adi Shankaracharya took the initiative of promoting the doctrine of Advaita Vedanta, which is based on the concept of non-duality. The beliefs and philosophies of Adi Shankaracharya formed the base for the Smarta tradition or Smartism.

Adi Shankaracharya founded four *Mathas*, one at Sringeri in Karnataka in the south and the others at Jyotirmath (Joshimath) in Uttarakhand in the north, Puri in Orissa in the east and Dwarka in Gujarat in the west. For each *Math*, he gave responsibility to one of his disciples.

He believed as he stated, 'Loud speech, profusion of words, and possessing skillfulness in expounding scriptures are merely for the enjoyment of the learned. They do not lead to liberation.'

VIVEKANANDA

Swami Vivekananda (January 12th, 1863 - July 4th, 1902) is one of the most inspiring personalities of India, who did a lot to make India a better place to live in within a short span of time, he achieved a lot and went a long way in serving humans. He was the principal disciple of Sri Ramakrishna Paramhansa.

It is Swami Vivekananda who can be attributed the credit for laying the foundation for the establishment of Ramakrishna Mission and *Math* that are actively involved in carrying out philanthropic works. The National Youth Day that is celebrated on the 12th of January every year is dedicated to Swami Vivekananda, as it is on this day that this impressive personality was born. His influence led to the introduction of Vedanta philosophy in America and England.

His efforts were acknowledged even by noted Indian leaders such as Mahatma Gandhi and Subhash Chandra Bose. Subhash Chandra Bose called him 'the maker of modern India'. According to Gandhiji, it was the influence of Swami Vivekananda that his love for his country increased thousandfold. He deserves major credit for giving the nation a modern vision.

Before turning into a monastic, Vivekananda was called by the name

Narendranath Dutta. He was born as the son of Viswanath Dutta and Bhuvaneswari Devi on January 12, 1863 in Shimla Pally, Kolkata, West Bengal. This gifted child started meditating at a very early age. Even as a child, he was an all-rounder. He was outstanding at studies, games and other extra-curricular activities. In the year 1879, he joined Presidency College for pursuing higher studies. After one year, he learnt philosophy from Scottish Church College, Calcutta. It was in this college that he got to know about Sri Ramakrishna of Dakshineswar.

The Ramakrishna Mission was founded by Swami Vivekananda, the chief disciple of Sri Ramakrishna Paramhansa on the 1st of May in the year 1897. The Vivekananda Ramakrishna Mission is actively involved in missionary as well as altruistic works such as disaster relief. The disciples who serve the mission consist of both monastics and householders. Its headquarters are based near Kolkata, India.

Swami Vivekananda was a great social reformer and a very inspiring personality. He was the pride of India. He made an immense contribution to purify the souls of people. He always said that God dwells inside every heart. He was of the opinion that, a person who cannot see God in poor and unhealthy people, but claims to see God in the idol, is not a true worshipper.

He compiled a number of books on the four Yogas, namely Raja Yoga, Karma Yoga, Bhakti Yoga and Jnana Yoga. His best literary works include the letters written by him, which have a lot of spiritual value. He maintained a very simple style of writing, so that laymen, for whom the message is meant, are able to understand his each and every word. He was not just actively involved in writing, but also was a great singer and composed several songs.

On July 4th, 1902, at a young age of 39, this great man left for his heavenly abode. The Swami had complete faith in God and did forego all worldly things. He believed that the three requisites for success are perseverance, patience and purity. If you think negative, then only negative things will happen in your life. Always think that you can do it, only then you'll be able to do it. Be optimistic in life. Strength is something that we need most in our lives. People, who are not strong enough to deal with the tough situations, finally land into trouble and misery. Swami Vivekananda said that weakness is the root cause of ignorance and ignorance leads to misery.

5 Cinematics

Indian film industry is the largest film industry in the world and every year more than 1000 films are produced in India. Indian cinema has made its mark all over the world. Indian actors are in demand in Hollywood movies, and leading Indian stars are popular in far flung corners of the world. Indian cinema has a history of nearly 100 years and has become an integral part of Indian society and culture.

Film With Most Number of Songs

Madan Theatres' Indra Sabha with seventy-one songs is the film with most number of songs. The film was made in 1932 and the director of the film was J.J. Madan. The plot of the film revolves around a benevolent king whose moral character is tested by celestial powers. They cause an apsara (a fairy) to appear before the king as a fallen woman begging for mercy. Indra Sabha was based on a play written by Sayed Aga Hasan Amanat. The film had two singers, Master

Nissar and Jehanara Kajjan. The other cast of the film included Abdul Rehman Kabuli and Mukhtar Begum.

First Colour Film Made in India

First colour film made in India was *Kisan Kanya* in the year 1937, although the trend of colour films began very late. The film was produced by Imperial Film Co. and was directed by Moti B. Gidwani. The film's music was composed by Ram Gopal Pandey. The film had ten songs, which were released by Gramophone Records. The storyline of the film featured an exploitative landlord and a good peasant, Ramu who is accused of murdering the landlord. The film was coloured using the Cinecolour process imported by Imperial Film Co. Kisan Kanya had a run time of 137 minutes and its main star cast included Padmadevi, Jillo, Ghulam Mohammed, Nissar, Syed Ahmed, and Gani.

First Indian to Get an Oscar

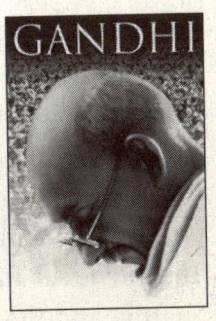

Bhanu Athaiya was the first Indian to get an Oscar. She won the award for the Best Costume Designer for Richard Attenborough's film Gandhi in 1982. Bhanu Athaiya has been associated with the Hindi film industry for more than fifty years. She was born as Bhanumati Annasaheb Rajopadhye in Kolhapur in Maharashtra. She married Satyendra Athaiya, a poet and lyricist for the Hindi film *Swades* (2004).

India's First Talkie Film

India's first talkie film was *Alam Ara* (Light of the Universe). The film was released on March 14, 1931 at Majestic Cinema in Bombay. *Alam Ara* was made under the banner of Imperial Movietone. It was produced and directed by Ardeshir Marwan Irani. The film was based on a successful Parsi play of the same name, written by Joseph David. The 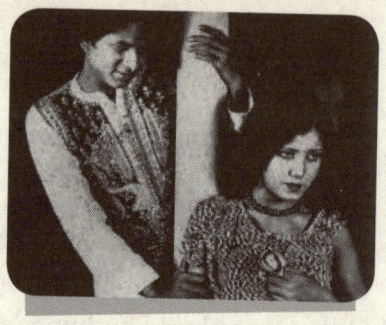 star cast of *Alam Ara* included some of the popular stars of the silent era like Prithviraj Kapoor, L.V. Prasad, W.M. Khan, Master Vithal and Zubeida. *Alam Ara* exploited the technological wonder of sound to the full. It had opulent sets and made rich use of music, song, and dance. *Alam Ara* had seven songs. The film took two months to complete. There were several technical hitches in sound recording. At that time there were no sound proof stages and most of the film was shot indoors and during night. Since the film was shot close to a railway track, the unit had to wait till the trains ceased to operate to begin the shoot.

Longest Hindi Film Song

The song '*Ab tumhare hawale watan saathiyon*' in the film by the same name is the longest Hindi film song. The length of the song is twenty minutes and the song is featured in three installments in the film. The song is sung by Sonu Nigam, Udit Narayan, and Kailash Kher and is written by Sameer. The music of the song is composed by Anu Malik.
The movie *Ab Tumhare Hawale Watan Saathiyon* is directed by Anil Sharma and the star cast of the film includes Amitabh Bachchan, Akshay Kumar, Bobby Deol, and Divya Khosla. *Ab Tumhare Hawale Watan Saathiyon* belongs to the genre of patriotism and the basic plot of the film revolves around the theme of fight against terrorism.

First Woman Music Director in Indian Film Industry

Jaddan Bai, mother of famous actress Nargis, was the first woman music director in Indian film industry. Jaddan Bai made a film *Talash-e-Haq* in the year 1935 and composed the music for it herself. In the same year Saraswati Devi scored the music for Mumbai Talkies' *Jawaani Ki Diwani*.

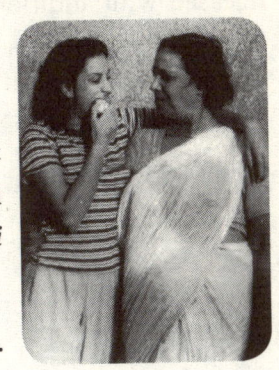

Jaddan Bai was a struggling artiste in Calcutta. It was the legendary singer K.L. Saigal who noticed her talent and encouraged her. So, from a gramophone singer, Jaddan Bai became an actress, music director and film producer.

First Indian Feature Film

Raja Harishchandra was the first full-length Indian feature film. The film was directed by Dhundiraj Govind Phalke (better known as Dadasaheb Phalke). The film was based on the legend of Harishchandra. Dadasaheb Phalke was greatly influenced by the style of painter Raja Ravi Verma in the making of *Raja Harishchandra*. The film was shown to a select audience on April 21, 1913 and was formally released on May 3 the same year at the Coronation Theatre in Bombay, where it ran for twenty-three days. *Raja Harishchandra* tells the tale of a virtuous monarch who donates his kingdom and sells himself into penury. The film was adapted from a successful stage production. It had subtitles in Hindi and English and featured male actors in the female roles.

First Indian 3D Movie

Chota Chetan was the first Indian 3D Movie. The film was made under the banner of Navodaya Films in 1984. *Chota Chetan* was a huge box office success and earned around Rs 60 crore during 1984-

85. The film also won the President's Gold Medal. The movie was re-released with additional footage and digital sound upgrade during 1998 and amassed Rs 50 crores during that period.

The Woods Of Film Worlds Around India

Bollywood: The biggest film industry in the country, it has been named after 'Bombay', from where it operates. Traditionally, it has been ruled by stars, but this year has seen scripts, scriptwriters and directors take centre stage, with many performer-actors rising in popularity.

Kollywood: The Tamil film industry is named after Kodambakam, an area in Chennai, which used to be the hub of all filmi activity in Tamil Nadu. Kollywood has always been known for idol worshipping. The Konkani film industry is also named thus, after the language. April 24, 1950, saw the first Konkani film release and this date, ever since, has been celebrated as the Konkani Cinema Day.

Tollywood: The Telugu film industry, which is one of the bigger ones in the country, is named after the language of Andhra Pradesh. This industry is known for making complete commercial entertainers.

If Telugu has inspired the name in Andhra, in Bengal, it is the area of Tollygunge that is responsible for it's name. An industry that's known to produce the most 'quality' films, it is synonymous with directors who've altered the course of parallel cinema in India like Satyajit Ray.

Sandalwood: Considering the fact that Karnataka has many sandalwood forests, one doesn't have to look too far to spot the inspiration. The industry has produced many matinee idols, but the names that have made a national mark are directors like Girish Kasaravalli, MS Sathyu and Girish Karnad.

Mollywood: Kerala's film industry is called Mollywood because of Malayalam language. This industry is also known for its art house cinema. Just like Kerala, Maharashtra's film industry has been christened Mollywood because of its operating language Marathi. This industry has a right mix of class and mass.

Gollywood: Gujarat's film industry is called so because of its regional language, Gujarati. This is one of the older industries with its first film dating back to 1932.

Pollywood: No prizes for guessing this one. The Punjabi film industry takes its name from the language. Punjabi films also date back a long time. Recent years have seen a revival of the industry, with many popular Punjabi Bollywood actors doing films in their native tongue.

6 All Four Sides

Delhi

Indeed, to know amazing India one has to understand the very 'threshold' of this country: It is believed that the name Delhi is derived from Dilli, a corruption of dehleez or dehali—Hindi for 'threshold'—and symbolic of city as a gateway to the Indo-Gangetic Plain. It is the political epicenter of political India. Delhi lives, breathes, eats and sleeps politics.

The social rank in this city is measured by political power. A young upcoming politician is several rungs higher than a flourishing lawyer. In fact well-to-do lawyers at present would like to taste the pie of politics these days. All and sundry, including those who walk the corridors of aristocracy long to go where power walks the talk, the Indian parliament. If one creates an almanac of who's who of Delhi, Bollywood does not feature much. Perhaps the the top ten celebrities here would have four politicians, six writers, painters and performing artists. The film stars, too, must perform on the political stage to win the attention of the capital of India.

The social lifestyle is the behest of politics, accompanied by the relevant status symbol. The scheming and gossiping amidst the elite often happens behind peaceful-looking bungalows. It doesn't have a hotel culture where one is to be seen or heard. There are some exclusive clubs of mostly retired bureaucrats that are vibrant with the bottom line, 'lend me your ears,' as whispers make the rounds. Symbols are flaunted in this city: cars with red beacons that flaunt status rather than utility. If the make is of a foreign car the more is the impact. The small 'people car' holds no ground. Now to be the savvy kind one has to flaunt the latest smartphones.

Night life in Delhi is almost dead. Even late evenings are determined by political hues. Delhi may bulge with museums, the hum of performing arts and the groan of historical monuments. Politics does have to come up to flavor the conversations at high tea and dinner gatherings, be it modest or grand. Whatever be the menu it will not get spiced up without a garnishing of political gossip. If one wants to see a caricature of Delhi life one has to visualize men standing drinking whisky, the women sitting chattering in the corners about the latest in vogue, food gobbled down hastily after midnight. Then everyone goes straight home. Lunchtimes, long light evenings and weekends, when club-life might blossom, are similarly popular. Clubs here lack the warmth where families and friends bubble in the weekends. An escape to a farm house- a farm out here has nothing to do with collecting warm hens' eggs for breakfast; it is a country house set in several acres with immense snob value.

In this part of the world, political influence matters. There is a lot of 'namesmanship' out here, dropping names of knowing the Jones' and the who's who in the political corridors. Influence can make one hop, skip and jump the line to get through the hoops to move across the labyrinth of government bureaucracy which baffles even its administrators. The scenario here demands powers of patience, persuasion, intrigue, name-dropping and 'baksheesh'. This chess-like site makes most MPs desert their constituencies and spend a quantum of their time in Delhi to carry back tell-tale anecdotes that they have qualified to be in the inner circle of influence. Besides the bureaucratic mire, there is a need for political muscle flexing. Delhi is the very place where the power is.

There are now twenty-nine states and seven Union Territories and Special Areas (of which Delhi is one). With life dominated by politics whose juicy tentacles stretch out to dust roads of many a rural village, electioneering is a major event. It is as colourful as a religious festival and laced with much show business. The symbols that do the round and paint the back drop are among many: the hand, the lotus, the wheel with regional symbols like the wicker lantern and of course the sickle. Election time is for politicians to scurry from one venue to another with surfeit of promises, roaring around the country-side in cavalcades of tooting cars, and if there is a helicopter it adds more brand value. Film stars are wheeled to add a million dollar smile drawing crowds who soon after vanish back to a celluloid world. But their presence seldom reflects itself in the votes. However, in the south, actors stand themselves with success. Election Day is a day of colours. Women dress in their Sunday best. There is plenty of dancing and music which turns into frenzy after the results are out. If the political decibels are too much, one can lose oneself in the Mughal architecture scattered in and around Delhi. For a taste of the old Muslim city, there are the alleys of Old Delhi and Nizamuddin. Delhi is a combination of two worlds—the old and the new.

If you look for something in between you will find none.

Delhi is made up of fifteen cities right from the 11th to the 20th centuries. There is little left of the early cities.

RAJASTHAN

Here lies classic fantasy of India at its best. Palaces built on dreams glow here amidst the fiery desert and setting sun. There are treasure trove bazaars of jewellery, precious stones, enameling, embroidery and mirror-work. Colour is further added by the attire and shy giggles of women here. They are dressed in splashes of raspberry pink, saffron, red and tangerine. Their noses, ears and toes are weighed down with silver jewellery. Swathed in long, tomato-red tunics and turbans they sing bhopas (folk ballads) about Rajasthani heroes and lovers. The maharajas' shadows still lengthen here. The locals still belong to the order and show love and respect to their maharaja. The remnants remain and some even elect him/her into the Indian parliament. The Desert Festival at Jaisalmer is vibrant with camel polo, camel races and desert music and dance. The traditional music, folklore, ritual and crafts

thrive across the state. The most familiar musician is the itinerant bhopa (balladeer), originating from Marwar. He sings and dances, clad in vermillion with a matching saffron turban. He dances along with his heavily veiled wife and often his young song playing his rawanhatta  stringed indstrument with a short bow tinkling with bells. There is Papuji ki Phad (scroll painting ballad) to elaborate upon each scene as they sing heroic poetry and mime dance, holding an oil lamp up to each intricately painted scene as the story of Pabuja unfolds. The subject is a 13th century hero from Rathore and performances of his deeds are supposed to remove evil influences from home. During festivals wealthier women dance the ghoomar in streets and villages, moving round in circles and twirling their ghongras or very full skirts. Men dance the gair to the beat of chang drum. This dance is much  faster, the dancers twisting and turning as they strike each others' sticks. Teratal or thirteen cymbals is a dance where men sing while women dance playing the thirteen cymbals tied over their bodies. A man fitted with a dummy silk horse to his waist dances the lok nritaka to the beat of his partners' drums. A folk musician plays the morchang (like a Jew's harp). A man is dressed up as a monkey amuses passers by; another as Hanuman, the monkey-god, howls and chatters and mimics his audience. Acrobats walk the tightrope or bend an iron bar with their foreheads. The nomadic Kalbelia tribe of snake charmers, the women heavily bejeweled, sing, dance and play the been or punji, made of gourd to entice the snake' posion sacs and reurn them to the wild when the sac refills.

The Kanjuri wears a tight pyjama, flowing skirt and conical hat, and calls himself both Radha and Krishna at once, singing songs about them as he moves from door to door. And there are puppeteers and all sorts of bhopas, some with bells, others playing the mashak (like a Scottish bagpipe) and others peforming feats like piercing a needle through the tongue.

Dried, crushed leaves of myrtle or rather mehendi are painted on women's feet and hands. A good design improves one's fortunes. A combination of applied lacquer and engraving to decorate brass trays, bowls, dishes and vases—the grander pieces of which are silver or gold-plated add to the celebration. Mojadis (slippers) often made of camel skin, are decorated with embroidered designs, the cobbler working in his bazaar shop.

Bandhani is a type of tie-dye textile decorated primarily by plucking the cloth with the fingernails into many tiny bindings that form figurative designs. The term bandhani is derived from the Sanskrit word banda ('to tie'). Today most Bandhini-making centers are situated in Gujarat, Rajasthan, Sindh, Punjab region and in Tamil Nadu where it's known as *Sungudi*.

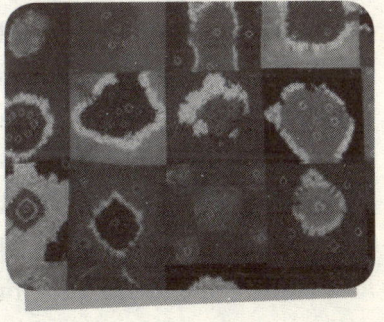

Block Printing-A block maker or a carpenter who specializes in block making is called 'Bhatt-ghar' in Rajasthan. Here Bhatt implies block and the ghar implies the carver. The block printers of Saanganer get most of their blocks made in Purani Basti in Jaipur. Those blocks that need special technical inputs are usually sent to Farukhabaad, Sitapur,

Meerut or Pilakuan in UP or Pethapur in Gujarat. Finesse in flowers-petal designs, curves and delicacy are the prime specialities of Saanganer prints. The curvature of flowers in the 'bootas' is generally shown on the right side. Different types of floral patterns are displayed in 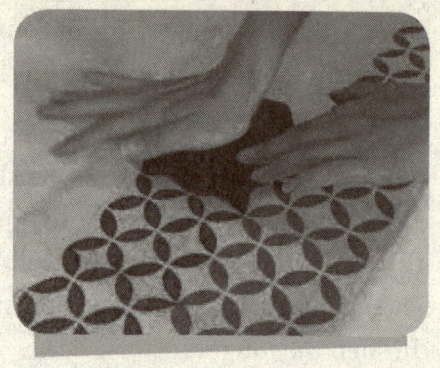 the form of a 'bel' (a border), in a stylized manner.

Some of the flowers used in the prints are roses, rosettes, lotuses, lotus buds, sunflowers, lilies, 'champa' 'canna' 'nergis', marigolds etc. Various other flower-based creations are also found in old Saanganeri prints. Other flowers used are locally known as sosan, gainda, gulmehendi, javakusum, guldaudi, kachnar, jatadari lily, kaner, kanna, gullala. Sosan and gullala prints are probably very suitable to Saanganeri style of printing, therefore they are used in various forms.

In booties, generally, only one type of flower-petal and bud creations are found; for example: Badaam (almond), Paan (beetle leaf), mukut of kalanga. While printing a sari, if the booti is of sosan flower then the bel will also be of sosan flower and a big boota of the same flower is usually done on the Pallav (the decorative edge of the sari, which is displayed by the women, and left hanging from the shoulders). Hence, for printing one sari, a large number of blocks need to be made. By printing different booties together, the Saanganeri 'Cheepas' have portrayed excellent knowhow. Sometimes more than three flowers are fitted beautifully in a single 'booti' e.g. in 'Latkan booti' (banana tree), sosan tree and saro tree collected and assembled beautifully in one pattern. The designs are named according to the flowers or plant pattern, from which the designs were originally inspired.

Khari printing - Khari or Chamki print is traditional printing and dyeing work, the roots of which are found in Rajasthan, India. Khari print work has earned immense fame in the past decades. This art of printing enhances the look of the fabrics, even the plainest textile.

Also known as Tinsel Printing, khari printing has been a long tradition in Rajasthan and originally this art of decorating textiles was extensively applied to the royal costumes and the articles that were used in royal kingdoms. This art work is today practised all over Rajasthan, Jaipur, Barmer, Jodhpur, Udaipur and Ajmer. Khari printing, in gold and silver, was developed to simulate the look of rich brocade and embroidery.

Mumbai

Often referred to as the 'Gateway of India,' Mumbai is a place that is characterized by colour, energy and life. It is an extremely busy place to live in, where different people from various cultures, religions and economic backgrounds converge to carve a path for themselves in a city that has come to be known as 'the city of dreams.'

Mumbai is often described as a place of contrasts and this is never more evident than in the stark divides between the rich and the poor. Slums and shanties are juxtaposed next to the multi-million pound homes of the rich and famous, sleek limousines glide past overcrowded double-decker buses and the bling on display in the glitzy shop fronts is obscured by homeless beggars and pavement stalls. Yet, despite these differences, the people of Mumbai exist peacefully, permeating an attitude of unity and fortitude.

Many expatriates may approach their impending relocation to Mumbai as a necessity that is to be endured, as opposed to embraced. However, there is much more to this fascinating city than power cuts, congestion, poverty, red tape and pollution. After living here for some time, one will slowly start to realize that the city is much more organized than it may first seem, albeit in a different way than that one may find in the West. One may also discover the heart of the Indian people and warm up their incredibly friendly nature and willingness to help.

Both gritty and glamorous, Mumbai seems to embody the personality of current day India. From the hip and trendy cocktail bars and after-hours clubs in Bandra and Colaba, to the hawker stalls stocked with patties, puris, kebabs and lassis, there is something on offer for everyone and an experience that will live with you forever.

Delhi and Mumbai are India's version of Washington and New York. A cynical India may call it the 'cheap imitation of Manhattan'. Indian single working women can lead a more liberated life there than elsewhere in the country, even in Delhi. Top Indian businessmen, merchants, dealers, actors make rounds here. Gujaratis, Parsees and Goans contribute to the immigrant population of nine million. In addition, there is a floating population of other Indians and foreigners, some working and some just having a good time here. For the Bombay rich, the coffers of rupees are emptied and replenished quickly; for the poor arriving with dreams, the rupees are few and life is squalid. One part of Bombay is ostentatiously rich; it also possesses India's largest slum, Dharavi, where people live in an area of 175 hectares only.

The city is the country's financial, industrial, commercial and trading centre. It has 15 per cent of India's factories, 45 per cent of her textile mills, handles 50 per cent of her foreign port traffic is responsible for a third of her income-tax receipts. The cash economy, known as 'black money' strives here like nowhere else. Nothing happens with out the 'black'!

The city has the highest cost of living in India, the largest film industry in the world, and property values on par with New York. It is the centre of the Indian gold and diamond markets, the best night life, and is the only Indian city to have an extensive network of good restaurants.

From Monday to Saturday, Bombay is action-packed. Deals are struck. Piles of rupees are made; more piles are spent. The streets are littered with jostling businessmen. Merchants and traders race to keep up supplies in shops and markets. Well organized beggars earn family wage at traffic lights. On Sunday, Bombay is silent except for the sound of the cricket bats on maidans.

The Mumbai Ganesh festival is one of the biggest celebrations in the city. Ganesh Chaturthi also known as Vināyaka Caturthi, Ganēśa Caturthī or Vināyaka Cavithi is the Hindu festival celebrated in

honour of the elephant-headed god, Ganesha. Chaturthi means 'fourth day' or 'fourth state'. Celebrations are traditionally held on the fourth day of the first fortnight (Shukla Chaturthi) in the month of Bhaadrapada in the Hindu calendar, usually August or September in the Gregorian calendar. The festival generally lasts ten days, ending on the fourteenth day of the fortnight (Anant Chaturdashi).

The festival is celebrated in public and at home. The public celebration involves installing clay images of Ganesha in public pandals (temporary shrines) and group worship. At home, an appropriately-sized clay image is installed and worshiped with family and friends. At the end of the festival, the idols are immersed (and dissolve) in a body of water such as a lake or pond.

It is celebrated throughout India, especially in Maharashtra. There is a grand celebration in the state of Maharashtra by traditional instruments called dhol and tasha. It is also celebrated in the other parts of India such as Gujarat, Karnataka, Telangana, Tamil Nadu, Kerala, Andhra Pradesh, Goa, Odisha, Madhya Pradesh, Chhattisgarh and other parts of western and southern India. Abroad, Ganesh Chaturthi is observed in the Terai region of Nepal and by the Hindu diaspora in the United States, Canada and Mauritius.

Every city has its own slangs, and in Mumbai it is famously called Tapori or 'Bambaiya (Mumbaiya) Language' which is not so polite if you understand Hindi, but Mumbai local people know it well and many a times use it commonly at public places, markets etc. in the city sometimes he/she enjoys the rough  talks. *Ek Dum Jhakaas Bidu* means you going perfect; *Bole Toh* means I mean; *Waat Lag gayi* means I'm in a kind of problem created; *Shaane* is a bad way of referring to a person as 'smarty'; *Locha Hogaya* or *Lafda Hogaya* is when things get messed up or there is some problem etc.

Underworld slang of Mumbai is changing: Khokha is archaic, so is peti. According to the new mafia lexicon, peti (Rs 1 lakh cash) has been replaced with haath and khokha (Rs 1 core) with kaan. A policeman is now referred to as a bidi. In the past, they were called pandu and thulla. Though gangs keep changing codes almost every three to four years, the cops have their khabris (informants), who help them decode the language jhadoo (broom), had been renamed guitar. A revolver and a pistol, which was earlier called a chakri and cassette, was till recently referred to as Ma and Bacche. The underworld would never use the word cash, currency or paise/rupiah on the phone. Earlier they called money as kagaj and now they refer to it as lottery. If a policeman has to be bribed, the gang member would be instructed, *Guldasta* (bouquet) *de do usko*. If they have to talk about making a 'fake passport', they would refer to it as puttha or a chidiya. A mobilephone, earlier called a kauva (crow), is now termed as hathwala.

STREET FOOD OF MUMBAI

People of Mumbai cut across barriers of class, religion, gender and ethnicity are passionate about street food. Street food of Mumbai is the food sold by hawkers from portable stalls in Mumbai. It is one of the characteristics of the city. The city is known for its distinctive street food. Although street food is common all over India, it is noted in Mumbai because people from all economic classes eat on the roadside almost round the clock and it is sometimes felt that the taste of street food is better than restaurants in the city. Many Mumbaikars like a small snack on the road in the evening.

Vada Pav is noted as the most popular street food in Mumbai. Other noted street foods in Mumbai include Panipuri, Bhelpuri, Sevpuri, Dahipuri, Sandwiches, Ragda-pattice, Pav Bhaji, Chinese bhel, idlis and Dosas, all of which are vegetarian. In terms of non-vegetarian offerings omelette-pav, kebabs and fish are found on Mumbai streets. Other popular street food items include Misal Pav (spicy curry made of sprouted moth beans which is eaten with pav, an Indian bread), and vegetable frankie (a popular and cheaper version of wraps and rolls). Kulfi (a type of ice cream) and Gola (type of ice cone) are among the desserts and coolants found on Mumbai streets. Tea vendors cycle around the city, selling the beverage hot on the streets. Street vendors normally remain unaffected by general strike calls and do business all year around.

Calcutta: Kolkata

The Calcuttan optimistically says, it is a city that is alive; the 'City of Joy'. The fabric of old Calcutta is decaying. The golden rule in Calcutta is 'the earlier the better'. As people, traffic and humidity increase, movement and energy slow down. There is bellowing of horns and choked up traffic. The humidity of the city may not encourage exercise, but the Bengal sweets may demand it.  Nostalgia is the essence that dates back to the end of the 1960s.

Kolkata as they say is a city, Calcutta, an emotion. In the heart of Bengal, the city of Chaurangi Rolls, Victoria Memorial and the ever so popular Park Street, Calcutta prides itself in rich heritage and culture. The rustic art, elaborate cuisine and a culture of respect and love for knowledge are its epicenters.

Kolkata was not only the first city of British India, it was also the city that took to British and Western culture in a manner that the other metros of the country never did. And Kolkata has one of the largest Anglo-Indian populations in the world.

An Anglo-Indian (people of mixed British and Indian ancestry or people of European descent born in India) is an original Calcuttan. He/she is as old as the city itself. Job Charnock, the founder of Calcutta, was the father of three daughters by his Indian wife. The early settlers left their womenfolk at home and so in the 17th and early 18th centuries, it was not uncommon for the Englishman to marry an Indian wife and adopt Indian ways. His children 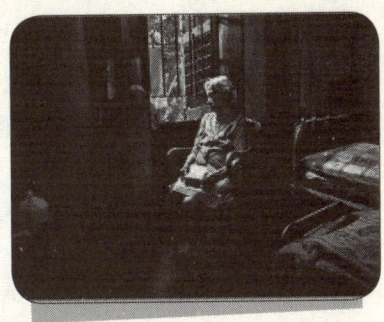 inherited his fortune and were sent home for education. The name Anglo-Indian was coined to describe an India-returned Englishman. It was not until the early 20th century that the word came to denote the mixed or Eurasian population in India.

Each Anglo-Indian family has its favourite recipes for prawn curry, vindaloo, jhal frazie and the all time favourite alu chop (potato rissole) to which the individual bawarchi (chef) adds his particular flavour. With Indian independence in 1947, the Anglo-Indian community felt insecure and there was mass exodus of those who wished to leave.

Many Anglo-Indians left the country in 1947, hoping to make a new life in the United Kingdom or elsewhere in the Commonwealth of Nations, such as Australia or Canada.

Those who remained were accepted as part of the Indian community. Not all agree that the job situation has improved, but there are many more opportunities. The Administrative and Defence Services hold Anglo-Indians in high positions.

From England and America, from Australia and Canada they come to visit the city of their birth. The younger generation comes in search of their roots.

The Bengali New Year or 'Poila Baisakh' (the first day of the month of Baisakh) is celebrated around 15 April on the basis of the lunar calendar. Visitors to homes are greeted with sweets, and trade establishments are decorated with auspicious garlands of marigold and aam leaves. Shop-owners and businessmen offer puja at Dakshineshwar Kali Temple and Kalighat Kali Temple in the morning with new ledgers (Halkhata). Businessmen also offer free sweets as a goodwill gesture on this day. It is celebrated by cultural programmes throughout Kolkata.

The Durga Puja festival, held in accordance to the lunar calendar of Bangabda around the first week of October, is the most vibrant time in Kolkata. Durga Puja is the most important, most popular and largest festival of Kolkata. More than 4500 pandals are set up in Kolkata and its suburbs, apart from a large number of old family pujas. Kolkata is famous for its vibrant nightlife and glamourous cultural activities during Durga Puja which continue till Kojagori Lakshmi Puja. Durga Puja has become Kolkata's biggest public

spectacle, art event and consumerist carnival. Streets, alleys, parks, gardens and most neighbourhoods glitter with lighting decorations. Pandal-visiting with friends, family members and relatives along with other festivities continue late into night. This Hindu religious festival commemorates the mythology of Goddess Durga and her trusty lion steed overpowering and killing the demon Mahishasura (buffalo-demon). The first ceremony takes place on Mahalaya, the day the Goddess was conceived, and ends on Bijaya Dashami (the victorious tenth day), the day the Goddess finally kills the demon in battle. Puja is performed only on the sixth to the tenth day. Kolkata celebrates Durga Puja with elaborate pandals—temporary decorative scaffolding serving the purpose of a temple—constructions on virtually every street. Crowds of people throng the streets of Kolkata all night; the number is purported to be a few million on the climactic eighth and ninth nights, possibly the second largest annual human conglomerate after the Hajj. On this festival, there is a practice of giving gifts—usually new clothes in the latest fashion in pre-puja get-togethers, and sweets at post-puja get-togethers (Bijaya Sammelani). The festival is commemorated by the publishing of annuals (Sharadiya or puja annual) by most Kolkata magazines and presses.

Today's puja goes far beyond religion and ritual worship. In fact, visiting the pandals recent years, one can only say that Durga Puja today is the largest outdoor art festival on earth. In the 1990s, a preponderance of architectural models came up on the pandal exteriors, but today the art motif extends to elaborate interiors, executed by trained artists, with consistent stylistic elements, carefully executed and bearing the name of the artist.

At the end of the six days long festival, the idol is taken in a procession of the deity to her home with her husband in the Himalayas. On Vijaya Dashami, the idols are carried out in large processions from all corners of the city to various ghats of the Ganga river. The processions end up with dhunuchi-naach, dance, maddening revelries and sindoor-khela after which the idols are immersed into the river amidst frolicking cheers. After this, in a tradition called Vijaya Dashami, families visit each other and sweetmeats are offered to visitors  (dashami is literally tenth day and vijay is victory).

Then there is Kali Puja. Kali Puja is primarily a Bengali Hindu festival, held in accordance to the lunar calendar around the first week of November. The Goddess Kali is worshipped at night on one night during this festival. Nights are lit up in Kolkata during Kali Puja, corresponding to the North Indian festival of Diwali (pronounced Dipabali in Bengali), where people light candles in memory of the souls of departed ancestors and decorate their homes with lights and rangoli. This is also a night of fireworks, with local youth burning sparklers and crackers throughout the night.

Dol, corresponding to the North Indian festival of Holi, is celebrated on account of the god Lord Krishna, and is supposedly coincident with the advent of spring. Holi is locally known here as Dolyatra or Basanta Utsab.

Costumes of Bengal represent the rich traditional culture of the region. While 'punjabi' form and 'dhoti' are common clothes among men, women love to wear sarees. Colourful clothes can be found in different cities, towns and villages throughout Bengal. Exciting clothes make the place really astonishing. These traditional and cultural

clothes are exported throughout India and other parts of the world. There are many importers who are interested in buying Bengali clothes.

In today's time, mostly youngsters attract and adorn western clothing like skirts, shirts, trousers, jeans, tops, t-shirts, etc. This commonly happens in cities like Kolkata and Dhaka. However, during festive seasons like Durga Puja you can find devotees wearing traditional clothing.

The typical Bengali fashion for women can be seen in saree (sari). This is one of the topmost traditional and widespread dresses for ladies. Generally, sarees from West Bengal are woven by silk or cotton. Salwar Kameez has also become a common dress among girls. These are available in various designs and colours in the street markets or shopping centers.

Bengal has its own style statement of sarees. Whenever we think of any Bengali saree, we visualize someone wearing crisp cotton, white sari with red border. Well, that traditional saree is none other than our good-old taant sarees—of course; the colour palette doesn't stick to the monotonous red and white combo. There are saris that bear different patterns and motifs with the floral, 'buti' and 'gamcha' designs dominating the scene.

Dhakai sarees were originally made in Dhaka before partition, this saree is one of the favorite saris of Bengals in all occasions—be it wedding parties, any Puja and even college farewells! Dhakai derives its nomenclature from Dhaka, where it was originally spun, and 'jamdani' refers to the typical design that the sari adorns. However, the 'korat' design is famous as well, and is more preferred than the former one by the youngsters.

Murshidabad Silk Saris: Some of the best silk sarees in India are made in Bengal. The history of silk saris in Murshidabad dates back to the 18th century when the East India Company set up two factories to produce silk.

Baluchari Saris: These saris get their nomenclature from Baluchar village in Murshidabad from where it originated. However, later, due to some geographical mishaps, the industry shifted from the silk-Mecca of east India to Bishnupur in the Bankura district of West Bengal.

Tussar silks: Although Tussar is produced in numerous areas in India, more than 40 per cent of it is produced in the Malda district of West Bengal. Tussar silk, a more textured one than the 'cultured' mulberry silk, aids in the making of numerous types of saris in Bengal. In fact, Baluchari saris are more often made with tussar silks than pure silk. However, apart from Balucharis, simple Tussar silks, in traditional Bengali 'buti' and 'pata' design is famous among women of all ages.

The 'bong' or Bengali has his own vocabulary. Yes, it's 'eesh!' the way Utpal Dutt used to say it. Awesome would be 'fatafati'. 'Kyabla' would mean the opposite of 'street smart'. 'Jaa taa' would literally mean 'this' and 'that'- it would mean something badly done. 'Iyarki peyechhe' literally means 'you think it's a joke!'; 'gondogol' is 'trouble;' 'pagal na mathakharab' would mean are you crazy; 'khetey diley shutey chaye' means 'feed food and he asks for a bed. When one is alarmed he says 'kheyeche' or 'morechey'.

Adda-An adda is a form of intellectual exchange among members, who were originally of the same socio-economic strata, but the process has democratized in modern times. It is most popular among the youths belonging to the so-called 'middle-class intelligentsia'. Adda was incorporated into the Oxford English Dictionary in 2004.

The platter is true Bengali food that has a bit of nostalgia of the Raj days. A 'kabirazi' cutlet is actually referring to 'coverage'; the sweet dish is a particular shape is called 'Lady Kenny' referring to Lady Canning. True Bengali food cannot be relished with spoons and forks.

'Khichuri' is the mother of all comfort foods. 'Khichuri' or Khichdi (a dish made up of rice and lentils) as it's known in many parts of India can be conjured up as a delicacy unlike in many parts of India where it is a basic meal served during ailment and sickness. In Bengal, Khichuri has attained a celebrity status, a cult-companion on a romantic rainy day.

West Bengal is famously known as the land of 'maach' (fish) and 'bhaat' (rice). Fried fish is fried raw fish without any marination or marinated with lil salt and turmeric. You can have it with rice and daal, could have it as a starter in a full course meal or anytime as a snack. Mutton curry is a hot and spicy lamb or mutton dish that is best served with Indian breads (roti, naan, parotha, etc.) or rice.

Kolkatans love to eat leafy vegetables. There are many leafy vegetables to choose from: spinach- commonly called 'palak' or 'palong saag', Malabar spinach: commonly called 'poi saag', fenugreek leaves: commonly called 'methi saag', water spinach: commonly called as 'kalmi saag', Amaranth: called 'note saag', Colocacia or taro leaves: called 'kachu'r pata or kachu'r lati', etc. A full course Bengali spread always

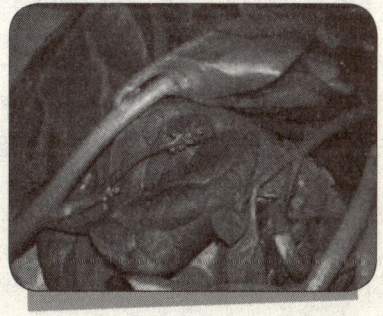

starts with a saag (leafy vegetable). And most of the plants grow as weed.

Bengali chicken curry is a basic chicken gravy recipe made with very little spices. It's almost most like a chicken stew with Indian spices, a must for a Sunday lunch. The chicken curry sure looks oily but it's the chicken fat.

Kolkata epitomizes the paan culture of India. In West Bengal, two types of betel leaves are produced, Bangla Patta and Mitha Patta. The latter is more popular among the connoisseurs.

Kolkata has always been a gourmet's paradise.

Roshogolla is a must for the sweet tooth of a Bengali and tourist; Sondesh-decorated with pistachios, almonds and saffron strands and prepared with milk, sugar and paneer; this mishti would simply melt in your mouth. There is home made milk-based payesh.

Chanachur-Chanachur is one of a kind very spicy-mix of dried ingredients. Kosha Mangsho (mutton curry)- Served with steamed rice, luchi (puri) and parothas, the velvety gravy with juicy pieces of meat, is a speciality.

Chicken Kabiraji-This, made with minced pieces of chicken, bread crumbs, ginger-garlic and egg, will fill you up for a while.

Then there is Mughlai Parotha-These deep fried parothas stuffed with egg and minced meats popular with a kind of twist is popular.

The three some: Kochuri–Torkari–Jilipi: This popular combo offers the combination of sweet,

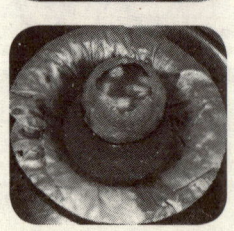

salt and spice. Phuchka- (called paanipuri in Mumbai and golgappa in Delhi) have their own signature taste in Kolkata. These tiny water-bombs with spice and masala are the cheap, yet filling.

Ghugni- With chanas and chickpeas is a quick snack.

Macher jhol (Fish-curry)—Macher jhol with rice is the staple food of this city, found almost everywhere in Kolkata.

Telebhaja-A perfect monsoon snack with cha/chai, ranging from beguni, phuluri, peyaji, alu'r chop to a variety of sinfully-crunchy, besan (corn-flour) covered street food!

Then there is Kathi Rolls, parathas rolled with kebabs, aloo, anda or egg and of course, Kolkata Biryani. This has a unique smell of desi ghee mixed with rich masalas and spices along with juicy, tender pieces of mutton cooked in rice. The unique feature of Kolkata Biryani is that it has a boiled egg and a boiled potato is an add-on in the platter of chicken and rice.

Pitha: Made from rice flour, this exquisite item can be both sweet and salty. Depending on the type, they are either fried or steamed.

Jhalmuri: Puffed rice or Muri mixed with peanuts, coriander and other spices, jhalmuri is an appetizing snack found in every street-corner of Kolkata.

Radha Ballavi/ Hinger Kochuri: A very popular breakfast dish of Kolkata, radha ballavis are fried, lentil-stuffed puris.

Mishti Doi: This doi beats any sort of frozen yogurt. It's a perfect blend of sugar and milk and curd.

The Bengali has his own terms for food and snacks. On a train 'time pass' is the peanuts that can be munched.

Varanasi - The Oldest City

Varanasi or Banaras or Kashi is a city famous for so many things, be it the 'nashta', 'paan', 'galiyan', 'ghats', temples or for being the home for Kashi Naresh or being one of the seven sacred cities in India or being one of the oldest inhabited city and it goes on.

The holy city lies in the northern belt of India, which clearly tells us that the temperature turns extreme whether its summer or winter. The legend says that Kashi was founded by Lord Shiva; Pandavas, the heroes of Hindu epic *Mahabharata* also visited the place in search of Shiva to cover for their sins during the Kurukshetra war. The earliest archeological evidence confirms that it is one of the world's oldest continually inhabited cities.

The name Varanasi is derived from from Varuna river and Assi ghat. The spiritual capital of India, it is the holiest of the seven sacred cities (Sapta Puri) in Hinduism and Jainism, and played an important role in the development of Buddhism.

Varanasi grew as an important industrial centre, famous for its muslin and silk fabrics, perfumes, ivory works, and sculpture. Buddha is believed to have founded Buddhism here around 528 BC when he gave his first sermon, 'The Setting in Motion of the Wheel of Dharma', at nearby Sarnath. The city's religious importance continued to grow in the 8th century, when Adi Shankara established the worship of Shiva as an official sect of Varanasi. Despite the Muslim rule, Varanasi remained the centre of activity for Hindu intellectuals and theologians during the Middle Ages.

Varanasi has been a cultural centre of North India for several thousand years, and is closely associated with the Ganges. Hindus believe that death in the city will bring salvation, making it a major centre for pilgrimage. The city is known worldwide for its many ghats,

embankments made in steps of stone slabs along the river bank where pilgrims perform ritual ablutions. The ghats in Varanasi are world-renowned embankments made in steps of stone slabs along the river bank where pilgrims perform ritual ablutions. The ghats are integral complements to the Hindu concept of divinity represented in physical, metaphysical, and supernatural elements. Varanasi has at least eighty-four ghats, most of which are used for bathing by pilgrims and spiritually significant Hindu puja ceremony, while a few are used exclusively as Hindu cremation sites. Of particular note are the Dashashwamedh Ghat, the Panchganga Ghat, the Manikarnika Ghat and the Harishchandra Ghat, the last two being where Hindus cremate

their dead. The Ramnagar Fort, near the eastern bank of the Ganges, was built in the 18th century in the Mughal style of architecture with carved balconies, open courtyards, and scenic pavilions.

Among the estimated 23,000 temples in Varanasi are Kashi Vishwanath Temple of Shiva, the Sankat Mochan Hanuman Temple, and the Durga Temple.

The Kashi Naresh (Maharaja of Kashi) is the chief cultural patron of Varanasi, and an essential part of all religious celebrations. An

educational and musical centre, many prominent Indian philosophers, poets, writers, and musicians live or have lived in the city, and it was the place where the Benares Gharana form of Hindustani classical music was developed. One of Asia's largest residential universities is Banaras Hindu University.

There is a tradition in India of chewing paan. It is most common in Uttar Pradesh. India is famous for the tradition of chewing pan (betel leaf). From ancient times paan was considered as part of the sacred Hindu rites and is offered to the deities of Hindus. Paan has great importance and is offered as a gesture of respect to guests in functions like wedding etc. The most commonly found types of paan include:

- Tobacco (tambaku paan): The paan bearing the powdered tobacco with spices.
- Betel nut (paan masala or sada paan and supari): Paan bearing the mixture of the chopped betel and other spices.
- Sweet (meetha paan): The betel leaf consists of fillings of coconut, fruit preserves and many spices. Cherry is also included in this. There is no tobacco in this paan.
- Trento (olarno paan): This is the paan that has the mint flavor and tastes like betel.

There is immense symbolism of paan. Betel leaf or paan plays a prominent role in the socio-religious life of the Hindus. No auspicious Vedic occasion moves ahead without a ritual involving paan in it. A popular folk marriage song of Eastern India describes the Himalayas as the birth-place of paan. It is believed that Lord Shiva and Parvati themselves had sown the seeds of paan in the Himalayan ranges.

In Hindu marriage ceremonies, a ritual called Briddhi-Sraddha is performed. As part of the ritual, the bride-groom invokes the resting souls of his ancestors; and in the presence of them all, he accepts the bride as his wife. At this instant, during the ancestral worship, thirty-two betel leaves or paan are compulsorily required.

Paan is also said to be the seat of Goddess Lakshmi, the famous Goddess of Wealth in Hindu religion. It is mentioned in Rajnirghantha that the tip of the leaf stands for longevity the basal portion is for fame while the middle portion is the seat of Goddess Lakshmi. So, chewing the middle portion of paan is a taboo to the Hindus.

CHENNAI

Chennai is a kind of doorway to South India. It is believed that Chennai is a miraculous gift the land of Tamil Nadu embraces. Chennai carries the legacy of rich cultural heritage imbibed in its fine arts, music and dance forms, people and cuisines. A cosmopolitan city, it mirrors confluence of diverse cultures nourishing within its boundaries.

A number of monuments across Chennai silently express the glorious history of the city, helping preserve its traditional art forms. The spirit of Chennai, vibrant culture and reminiscent traditions, all make the city wonderful and tremendously important as a part of Indian heritage.

Chennai, yesterday's Madras, remained under the influence of many great dynasties like the Pallavas, the Cholas, the Pandyas and the Vijaynagar Empire. From just being a fishing village known as 'Madraspatnam', the city became one of the most important cities of the country, though slowly and steadily.

Chennai is home to various religions. Be it Hindu, Muslims, Christians to Jains, Chennai has warmly welcomed them all. This metropolitan city, Chennai, is a breathing example of perfect confluence of traditional beliefs and modernity in one's life.

The capital city and metropolis Chennai is a wonder when it comes to language. Though Tamil enjoys the status of being the prime language in the city and the mother tongue, popularly articulated by the citizens of the city, however, people belonging to different regions have brought their native languages with them. Other spoken languages here are English, French, Portuguese, Dutch, Telugu, Urdu, Kannada, Bengali, Punjabi and Malayalam.

When it comes to hospitality and traditional food, Chennai makes a statement of its own. They serve number of traditional food items including sambhar, dosa, idli, rasam, coconut chutney, dry curry and kootu etc. with steamed rice on banana leaf, which is the traditional way of dining in Chennai. The city has multiple variants of cuisines for vegan as well as for non-vegetarians. That which steals the show is the rich Tamilian filtered coffee.

South Indian culture refers to the culture of the South Indian states of Tamil Nadu, Karnataka, Kerala, Andhra Pradesh and Telangana. The South Indian culture is essentially the celebration of the eternal universe through the celebration of the beauty of the body and motherhood. It is exemplified through its dance, clothing, and sculptures.

South Indian women traditionally wear the saree while the men wear a type of sarong, which could be either a white dhoti or a colourful lungi with typical batik patterns.

The saree, being an unstitched drape, enhances the shape of the wearer while only partially covering the midriff. In Indian philosophy, the navel of the Supreme Being is considered as the source of life and creativity. Hence by tradition, the stomach and the navel are to be left unconcealed. This makes the realization of sharira-mandala, where in Angikam bhuvanam yasya (the body is your world) unites with the shaarira-mandala (the whole universe), as expressed in the Natyashastra. The lungi or mundu or panchey (a white lungi with colourful silk borders in kannada), is worn by men.

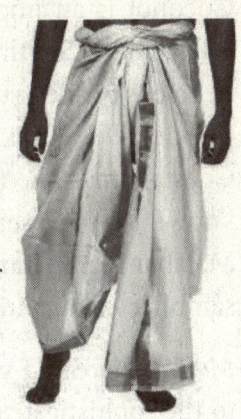

Traditionally, South Indian men do not cover their upper bodies. Sometimes, in a formal situation, a piece of cloth may cover the upper body. Certain temples in South India even ban men from wearing upper-body garments when inside the temple.

In Andhra and parts of north Karnataka men wear kachche panchey where it is tied at back by taking it between legs. A similar pattern is seen in women. All over the peninsular coastal region men wear coloured lungis and women wear saris in a manner of tying them at the back.

The Araimudi (araimuti) was worn by young Tamil girls. The Araimudi is a small silver metal plate, shaped like a heart or a fig leaf. 'Arai' means loin and 'mudi' means cover.

Food: The tradition of serving meals on plantain leaves endures in

South India, especially at formal events. Rice is the staple diet, with fish being an integral component of coastal South Indian meals. Coconut is an important ingredient in Kerala and coastal part of Karnataka of South India. In Andhra Pradesh food is characterized by delicious pickles, spicy aromatic curries and the generous use of chili powder. Dosa, idli, uttapam etc. are popular throughout the region. Coastal areas like the state of Kerala and the city of Mangalore are known for their seafood. Coffee is a preferred drink throughout the Malabar region. Tamil Nadu is well known for its idli, dosai, pongal, sambhar, vadai, puri. This is the common breakfast in Tamil families.

Music: There is a variety of music. It ranges from rural folk music to the sophisticated Indian classical music of South India known as Carnatic music (after Carnatic, the name by which south India was known in the earlier colonial days. Sarang Dev coined south Indian classical music as carnatic music). In Tamil Nadu, there is Tamil Pann, which is sung by Oduvars in temples. They sing the works of famous Tamil poets like Sambandar, etc. in various panns (another word for raagas).

Hindu Temple Music: The main instrument that is used in south Indian Hindu temples is the nadaswaram. It is said to have been created when the very first temple was established in South India. The nadaswaram and the thavil were played together in South Indian temples to create a periya melam ensemble. In South India, it is a sound of pride and majesty. For many temple traditions, periya melam is necessary for worshippers to feel spiritual presence.

Dance: The South Indian culture is celebrated in the elaborate dance forms of South India—Koodiyattam, Bharatanatyam, Oyilattam, Karakattam, Kuchipudi, Kathakali, Thirayattam, Theyyam, Bhuta Kola, Ottamthullal, Oppana, Kerala Natanam, Mohiniaattam and Yakshagana. Bharatanatyam is the celebration of the eternal universe through the celebration of the beauty of the body. This is done through its tenets of having a perfectly erect posture, a straight stomach, a well rounded and proportionate body mass—to the body structure, very long hair and curvaceous hips. These tenets bring to life the philosophy of Natyashastra, 'Angikam bhuvanam yasya' (The body is your world). This is elaborated in the araimandi posture, wherein the performer assumes a half sitting position with the knees turned sideways, with a very erect posture. In this fundamental posture of the Bharatanatyam dance, the distance between the head and the navel becomes equal to that between the earth and the navel. In a similar way the distance between the outstretched right arm to the outstretched left arm becomes equal to the distance between the head and the feet, thus representing the 'Natyapurusha', the embodiment of life and creation.

7 Snippets

A Floating Post Office

India has the largest postal network in the world with over 1,55,015 post offices. A single post office on an average serves a population of 7,175 people. The floating post office in Dal Lake, Srinagar, was inaugurated in August 2011.

Kumbh Mela Gathering Visible From Space

The 2011 Kumbh Mela was the largest gathering of people with over 75 million pilgrims. The gathering was so huge that the crowd was visible from space.

The Wettest Inhabited Place In The World

Mawsynram, a village on the Khasi Hills, Meghalaya, receives the highest recorded average rainfall in the world. Cherrapunji, also a part of Meghalaya, holds the record for the most rainfall in the calendar year of 1861.

Steel Wires Equal To The Earth's Circumference

Bandra Worli Sealink has steel wires equal to the earth's circumference. It took a total of 2,57,00,000 man hours for completion and also weighs as much as 50,000 African elephants. This is a true engineering and architectural marvel.

The Highest Cricket Ground In The World

At an altitude of 2,444 meters, the Chail Cricket Ground in Chail, Himachal Pradesh, is the highest in the world. It was built in 1893 and is a part of the Chail Military School.

Shampoo was invented in India, not the commercial liquid ones but the method by use of herbs. The word 'shampoo' itself has been derived from the Sanskrit word champu, which means to massage.

The Indian National Kabaddi Team Has Won All World Cups

India has won all five men's Kabaddi World Cups held till now and has been undefeated throughout these tournaments. The Indian women's team has also won all Kabaddi World Cups held till date.

Water On The Moon Was Discovered By India

In September 2009, India's ISRO Chandrayaan-1 using its Moon Mineralogy Mapper detected water on the moon for the first time.

Science day in Switzerland is dedicated to Ex-Indian President, APJ Abdul Kalam. The father of India's missile programme had visited Switzerland back in 2006. On his arrival, Switzerland declared May 26th as Science Day.

India's First President Only Took 50 Per cent Of His Salary

When Dr Rajendra Prasad was appointed the President of India, he only took 50 per cent of his salary, claiming he did not require more than that. Towards the end of his twelve-year tenure he only took 25 per cent of his salary. The salary of the President was Rs 10,000 back then.

The First Rocket In India Was Transported On A Cycle

The first rocket was so light and small that it was transported on a bicycle to the Thumba Launching Station in Thiruvananthapuram, Kerala.

India Has A Spa Just For Elephants

Elephants receive baths, massages and even food at the Punnathoor Cotta Elephant Yard Rejuvenation Centre in Kerala.

India Is The World's Second-Largest English Speaking Country

India is second only to the USA when it comes to speaking English with around 125 million people speaking the language, which is only 10 per cent of its population.

Amazing India Facts

Largest Number Of Vegetarians In The World

Be it because of religious reasons or personal choices or both, around 20-40 per cent of Indians are vegetarians, making it the largest vegetarian-friendly country in the world.

The World's Largest Producer Of Milk

India recently overtook the European Union with production reaching over 132.4 m tonnes in 2014.

The First Country To Consume Sugar

India was the first country to develop extraction and purifying techniques of sugar. Many visitors from abroad learnt the refining and cultivation of sugar from India.

The Human Calculator

Shakuntla Devi was given this title after she demonstrated the calculation of two thirteen digit numbers: 7,686,369,774,870 × 2,465,099,745,779 which were picked at random. She answered correctly within twenty-eight seconds.

Rabindranath Tagore Wrote The National Anthem Of India And Bangladesh

Rabindranath Tagore is credited not only for writing the Indian national anthem, Jana Gana Mana, but the Bangladeshi national anthem, Amar Sonar Bangla, as well. He was also offered knighthood by the British but refused the honour after the Jalianwala Bagh massacre.

Amazing India Facts

Dhyan Chand Was Offered German Citizenship

After defeating Germany 8-1 in the 1936 Berlin Olympics, Major Dhyan Chand, the wizard of hockey, was summoned by Hitler. He was promised German citizenship, a high post in the German military and the chance to play for the German national side. Dhyan Chand however declined the offer.

Freddie Mercury And Ben Kingsley Are Both Of Indian Descent

Freddie Mercury, the legendary singer of the rock band 'Queen' was born a Parsi with the name Farrokh Bulsara while the famous Oscar winning Hollywood star Ben Kingsley was born Krishna Pandit Bhanji.

Astronaut Rakesh Sharma Said India Looks Saare Jahaan Se Achcha From Space

Former Prime Minister Indira Gandhi asked the first Indian in space, Rakesh Sharma, about how India looked from space. His response was India's famous patriotic song, 'Saare Jahaan Se Achcha.'

Havell's Is Purely An Indian Brand And Named After Its First Owner

Though the company was bought for just 10 lakh rupees a long time ago and is now a multi-billion electrical goods company, it's an Indian company and is still named after its original owner, Haveli Ram Gupta.

Diamonds Were First Mined In India

Initially, diamonds were only found in the alluvial deposits in Guntur and Krishna District of the Krishna River Delta. Until diamonds were found in Brazil during the 18th century, India led the world in diamond production.

A Special Polling Station Is Set Up For A Lone Voter In The Middle Of Gir Forest

Mahant Bharatdas Darshandas has been voting since 2004 and during every election since then, a special polling booth is set up exclusively for him as he is the only voter from Banej in Gir forest.

Snakes and Ladders originated in India

Earlier known as Moksha Patamu, the game was initially invented as a moral lesson about karma to be taught to children. It was later commercialized and has become one of the most popular board games in the world.

Zero defect of Mumbai Dabbawalas

Dabbawalas can be found in the Indian city of Mumbai. The job of a dabbawala (box person) is to collect tiffin boxes from the house

of office workers, deliver it to their workplace and carry it back to the residence. These dabbawalas don't rely on computers to sort and group thousands of dabbas to be delivered at different areas in Mumbai. They rely on certain symbols and markings on the dabba to ascertain its delivery address. So there is a good chance that they end up delivering dabbas at the wrong address. But never do they go wrong. According to a report by Forbes Magazine, the dabbawalas make just one error in six million deliveries!

There is a village called Snapdeal Nagar in Uttar Pradesh

Shiv Nagar in Uttar Pradesh changed its name to Snapdeal Nagar, because the e-commerce company installed fifteen hand pumps in the village.

There is a species of shark known as the Ganges Shark that inhabits the River Ganga: Ganges Sharks are true river sharks, and are unfortunately critically endangered.

INDIA HAS THE WORLD'S FIRST HOSPITAL TRAIN.

The Lifeline Express is the world's first hospital on train. Started on 16th July, 1991, the train reaches the most rural parts of India and offers medical help.

The Oldest Brand In The World Is In India.

The healthy supplement Chyawanprash is known to be the oldest brand in the world. Originated since the Vedic period, it has been in continuous demand till date.

Isisaurus: Named after Indian Statistical Institute (ISI), the gigantic dinosaur's remains were found in Dongargaon Hill in Maharashtra. Isisaurus is one of the few dinosaurs ever to be dug up on the Indian subcontinent.

India's Road Network Is Long Enough To Loop Around The Earth Over 117 Times.

India's road network totals to 4.7 million kilometres!

The Country Houses The World's Most Expensive Home.

Antilia, the home of billionaire Mukesh Ambani is the most expensive home in the world. The twenty-seven story, 400,000-square foot skyscraper residence stands tall in Mumbai.

Molai Forest In Assam

This 1,360-acre forest located in Assam was planted by one man. In 1979, when Jadav 'Molai' Payeng was just sixteen years old he decided to plant some seedlings on a sandbar. For the next four decades he continued planting more and more seedlings, creating the large forest reserve that exists today.

Suicidal Birds In Jatinga

For over 100-years, birds have been flocking to Jatinga, a village located in Assam, to 'commit suicide.' Some people attribute this deeply depressing phenomenon to the birds becoming disoriented due to high wind speeds at high altitudes, although an official reasoning has not yet been proven.

100-Year-Old Underground Fire

This underground fire in Jharia, Jharkhand has been burning in the coalmines for at least a hundred years. The flames were originally detected in 1916, and ever since the mining department and railway authorities have been busy trying to put out the flames with no success.

The Village Of Twins

Kodinhi, Kerala Kodinhi, a village in Kerala, is home to 2,000 families and over 220 sets of twins—an abnormally high number per population. Even stranger, the number of twins is increasing every year.

Uttarakhand's Roopkund Lake

Uttarakhand's Roopkund Lake is home to a collection of human skeletons. Every year, when the snow melts the skeletons become visible again. Radiocarbon dating shows these skeletons are over thousand years old, although the reason so many bones ended up here in the first place remains one of India's many mysteries.

The HUGE Great Banyan Near Kolkata

The Huge Great Banyan tree is growing on the outskirts of Kolkata. The tree is two-hundred years old, and takes up around 14,500 square metres. It continues to grow beyond the 330-metre road that was built around its original circumference.

Amazing India Facts

Abandoned 'Cursed' Village Of Kuldhara, Rajasthan

Some two-hundred years ago, Kuldhara was home to more than 1,500 Paliwal Brahmins who had called the land home for over five centuries. Mysteriously, every single resident from Kuldhara's eighty-five distinct villages fled from their homes one night, it is said that they  left a curse on the land so that no one else would ever live there. To this day, the land remains deserted and is home to a collection of human skeletons. Every year, when the snow melts the skeletons become visible again. Radiocarbon dating shows these skeletons are over thousand years old, although the reason so many bones ended up here in the first place remains one of India's many mysteries.

First University

Takshila is said to be the first university in the world; it started around 700 BC.

Railways

Indian Railways employs more than 1.3 million people. That's more than the population of many nations.

Voters

More than 54 crore people voted in the 2014 General Election–more people than the population of USA, UK, Australia and Japan combined.

Births

Number of births in India every year is more than the total population of Australia, and many other nations.

Lonar Lake

Lonar Lake, a saltwater lake in Maharashtra, was created by a meteor hitting the earth. It is one of its kind in India.

A Unique Village

In a village called Shani Shingnapur in Maharashtra, people have been living in houses with no doors for generations. This is because they believe that whoever steals anything from this place will incur the wrath of Shani God and will have to pay for his/her sins very dearly. There is no police station in this village either.

Magnetic Hill

Magnetic Hill is a gravity hill located near Leh in Ladakh, India. The hill is alleged to have magnetic properties strong enough to pull cars uphill and force passing aircrafts to increase their altitude in order to escape magnetic interference.

Cursed River

Karmanasa River in India is considered to be a cursed river and it is believed that touching its water would ruin one's plans. There's hardly any development along this river. People around this river just eat dry fruits because cooking food would require water!

First Granite Temple

The first granite temple of the world, the Brihadeswara temple is

situated in Tamil Nadu. It was built during the 11th century, in only five years.

National Drink

Chai is India's national drink.

King of Fruits

India grows 1.2 million tons of mangoes every year, weighing equivalent to 80,000 blue whales.

Yoga

India gave the world Yoga that has existed for more than 5,000 years.

Martial Arts

Martial Arts was first created in India.

Renames and Respelled

THEN	NOW
United Provinces	Uttar Pradesh
Travancore-Cochin	Kerala
Madhya Bharat	Madhya Pradesh
Madras State	Tamil Nadu
Mysore	Karnataka
Uttaranchal	Uttarakhand
Orissa	Odisha
West Bengal	Paschim Banga
Assam	Asom
ANDHRA PRADESH	
Garthapuri	Guntur
Kandenavolu	Kurnool
Ellore	Eluru
Waltair	Visakhapatnam
Bezawada	Vijayawada
Cocanada	Kakinada
Masulipatam	Machilipatnam
Sikkolu	Srikakulam

Vikrama Simhapuri	Nellore
ASSAM	
Nowgong	Nagaon
Gauhati	Guwahati
Sibsagar	Sivasagar
GUJARAT	
Baroda	Vadodara
Broach	Bharuch
Karnavati	Ahmedabad
Cambay	Khambhat
Bulsar	Valsad
Suryapur to Surat	Himachal Pradesh
Simla	Shimla
Mandav Nagar	Mandi
GOA	
Panjim	Panaji
Sanquelim	Sankhali
KARNATAKA	
Bangalore	Bengaluru
Mysore	Mysuru
Mangalore	Mangaluru
Hubli	Hubballi

Tumkur	Tumakuru
Shimoga	Shivamogga
Belgaum	Belagavi
Bellary	Ballari
Gulbarga	Kalaburagi
Marcera	Madikeri
Bijapur	Vijayapura
Hospet	Hosapete
Chikmagalur	Chikkamagaluru

KERALA

Trivandrum	Thiruvananthapuram
Cochin	Kochi
Calicut	Kozhikode
Quilon	Kollam
Trichur	Thrissur
Cannanore	Kannur
Palghat	Palakkad
Alleppey	Alappuzha
Alwaye	Aluva
Cranganore	Kodungallur
Tellicherry	Thalassery
Badagara	Vatakara

Palai	Pala
Verapoly	Varapuzha
Cherpalchery	Cherpulassery
Koney	Konni
Sherthalai	Cherthala
MADHYA PRADESH	
Indur	Indore
Avantika	Ujjain
Bhelsa	Vidisha
Rassen	Raisen
Saugor	Sagar
Jubbulpore	Jabalpur
Bellasgate	Bheraghat
Ojjain	Ujjaini
Mandu	Mandavgarh
Viratnagari	Shahdol
MAHARASHTRA	
Bombay	Mumbai
Nasik	Nashik
Poona	Pune
Thana	Thane
Bhir	Beed

PUDUCHERRY	
Pondicherry	Puducherry
Yanaon	Yanam
PUNJAB	
Jullunder	Jalandhar
Ropar	Rupnagar
Mohali	SAS Nagar
Nawan Shahar	Shaheed Bhagat
RAJASTHAN	
Ajaymeru	Ajmer
TAMILNADU	
Tinnevelly	Tirunelveli
Tranquebar	Tharangambadi
Trichinopoly	Tiruchirapalli
Trinomalee	Tiruvannamalai
Madras	Chennai
Tanjore	Thanjavur
Karuvur	Karur
Tuticorin	Thoothukudi
Cape Comorin	Kanyakumari
Ootacamund	Udagamandalam
Conjeevaram	Kanchipuram

Virudupatti	Virudhunagar
Potonovo	Parangipettai
Mayavaram	Mayiladuthurai
UTTAR PRADESH	
Allygurh	Aligarh
Cawnpore	Kanpur
Banaras	Varanasi
Prayag	Allahabad
Noida	Gautam Budha Nagar
WEST BENGAL	
Calcutta	Kolkata
Burdwan	Bardhaman
Chinsurah	Hugli-Chuchura
TELANGANA	
Edlabad	Adilabad
Bhagyanagaram	Hyderabad
Elagandla	Karimnagar
Indur	Nizamabad
Palamuru	Mahabubnagar
Orugallu	Warangal

MORE SNIPPETS

- Hindi words choli (blouse) and pallu (end piece of a sari) has been derived from the names of Tamil dynasties viz. Cholas and Pallavas respectively.

- Samosas are banned in Somalia as they resemble the shape of the Christian Holy Trinity.

- In 1948, the Nobel Peace Prize was not awarded. It would have been awarded to Mahatma Gandhi, however, due to his assassination it was left unassigned in his honor.

- In 2004, Marvel Comics launched Spider Man India where Peter Parker was called Pavitr Prabhakar, Mary Jane as Meera Jain, Aunt May as Auntie Maya, Uncle Ben as Uncle Bhim.

Amazing India Facts

- Rumble-tumble was the Raj name for scramble egg; if tomatoes were added to rumble-tumble then it became craggy toast. Ox eyes were slices of fried bread with the centre cut out and replaced by an egg and then baked.

- Kheer is a popular sweet dish in North India; Payasam is its equivalent in South India.

THE INDIAN SAREE

- The Sari word is derived from Sanskrit 'Sati' and 'Shatika', which means 'strip of cloth'. It was corrupted to 'Sadi' and 'Sattika' in Prakrit, and then 'Sari' and 'Saree' in Hindi.

- 'Saree' has been referred in *Rigveda* as Hiranyadrapi, made from a shining, gold-woven cloth with border as pattas. Women of Vedic period used to wear a uttariya (upper garment), an antariya (lower garment) and a kayabandh (waistband). Saree was worn in form of a uttariya.

- According to great epic *Ramayana*, when Sita, the wife of Lord Rama is abducted by demon Ravana, she tears apart a piece of her saree and throws her anklets, bracelets and other jewellery tied in it.

- In great epic *Mahabharata*, when Dhushashan tries to strip the Draupadi, she calls to Lord Krishna, who increases the size of saree performing a miracle and Dhushashan fails in his wicked purpose. In this scripture, minicheri is mentioned, which is an interwoven saree embellished with pearls and glittering borders.

- According to Natya Shastra (200 BC and 200 AD) of Sage Bharata, the navel of Supreme Being is the source of life and creativity. Therefore, midriff is kept left bare by the sari.

- In ancient Jain and Buddhist scriptures, saree has been mentioned in Prakrit word 'Sattika'.

- In archeological excavation of Indus valley civilization period (2800-1800 BC), the statue of a priest wearing a saree has been found.

- In Ajanta cave sculpture and painting (2nd century BCE), several figures are portrayed wearing different types of sarees, which indicate that contemporary Indian artisans were well-versed of weaving the sarees in different techniques.

- Various sculptures of Gandhara, Mathura and Gupta schools of art (1st- 6th century) depict the goddesses and dancers wearing a saree. The saree used to be created in 'fishtail' design, which loosely covers legs and then flows in front of leg like a long, decorative drape.

- Banabhatta in his Sanskrit romantic work, *Kadambari* (first half of 7th century) describes the ladies wearing elegant drapery or sari.

- Saree has also mentioned in the ancient Tamil poetry *Silappadhikaram* of Ilango Adigal.

- Several ancient Hindu temples have been decorated with the wall carvings depicting the figurines sporting sarees.

- Popular Indian historical heroines like Kittur Chennamma (1778-1829), Lakshmi Bai, the Rani of Jhansi (1835-1858) and Belawadi Mallamma (17th century) battled with enemy troops on horseback wearing tightly tied sarees.

- Popular Indian painter Raja Raviverma (19th century) has painted various Hindu goddesses wearing sarees.

Indian Weddings

- Some Hindu families practise the custom of giving the bride a knife or some other sharp metal object to keep with her at all times from the time she gets engaged to the wedding day, to protect her from any unwanted male attention or advances.

- In many cultures and communities across India, it is actually considered good luck if it rains on the wedding day.

- Muslim weddings traditionally include a custom called 'meher'. It is a formal statement of a sum of money that the groom hands over to the bride. Meher is given in two parts, the first being handed over before the marriage is consummated and the second given in parts as cash, jewelery or property. This gift is for the bride to do with as she pleases.

- In the Punjabi community, the brides wear a 'Chudaa' (a set of red and white bangles) for a few months into the marriage, to bring them good luck in their new homes.

- Christian weddings are preceded by a fun ceremony called the bridal shower. This is an event usually hosted by the bride's female friends. It's a lively gathering of women, with music, dance and games. All guests bring gifts for the bride-to-be and give her their blessings for a happy married life. The bride serves a pink cake to everyone present with a piece of thimble hidden inside. It is believed that if an unmarried girl gets this piece of thimble, she will get married soon.

- During the oder days, in Kerala, the concept of a 'mock wedding ceremony' was prevalent in some communities. During this ceremony, the bride was married to a man who was a perfect astrological match for her. Since this was a mock marriage, the bride and groom could go their own separate ways after the ceremony was over.

- 'Mangala Snaanam' or the purification bath is a pre-wedding custom in many Indian communities. It is done at first light on the day of the wedding for the purification of the bride and groom's physical selves, before they begin wedding rituals.

- Sikh families have after wedding games to welcome the new bride to their families. One of them is the knotted string game, where the sister of the groom ties several knots in a long string and the bride and groom are supposed to use one hand each and work together to pry open the knots. It is believed that the sooner they untie the knots, the smoother their wedded lives will be.

- An old wives tale for the 'bidaai' ceremony states that if the bride sheds a tear or two, she will never cry again for the entire duration of her marriage.

- The Gujarati community performs a custom, where the mother of the bride tries to catch the groom's nose when the baraat arrives, to remind him that since he is now taking away her daughter, he will be responsible for her well-being and happiness.

- Sikh weddings have a pre-wedding 'vatna' ceremony, usually done a day before the wedding, where the women of the family apply a paste of haldi and besan to the bride's body, and sing traditional songs.

- As per tradition, both Hindu and Sikh brides, before taking the first step into their new homes, tilt over a vessel full of wheat. This is symbolic of the prosperity and abundance that a bride is believed to bring to her new home.

- Islamic weddings have their own versions of the purification bath, which is performed on the day of the Nikaah, or in some Muslim families, is a ritual performed every day, starting five days before the wedding. The bride may be accompanied by some women in the family amid music and dancers, making it a festive procession.